DISCARD

THE

JOSEPH

BLESSING

DESTINY IMAGE BOOKS BY JORDAN RUBIN

The Maker's Diet

The Maker's Diet Revolution

The Maker's Diet Transformation DVD and Study Guide

THE
JOSEPH
BLESSING

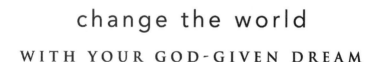

change the world

WITH YOUR GOD-GIVEN DREAM

JORDAN RUBIN & PETE SULACK

DESTINY IMAGE® PUBLISHERS, INC.
P.O. Box 310, Shippensburg, PA 17257-0310
"Promoting Inspired Lives."

Editorial assistance by Mike Yorkey (www.mikeyorkey.com).

Cover Design by: Prodigy Pixel

This book and all other Destiny Image and Destiny Image Fiction books are available at Christian bookstores and distributors worldwide.

For more information on foreign distributors, call 717-532-3040.
Reach us on the Internet: www.destinyimage.com.

ISBN 13 HC: 978-0-7684-0603-0
ISBN 13 Ebook: 978-0-7684-0604-7

For Worldwide Distribution, Printed in the U.S.A.
1 2 3 4 5 6 7 8 / 18 17 16 15 14

CONTENTS

1

THE START OF A DREAM

So here I (Jordan) am on a sunny spring morning at our ranch and farm in south-central Missouri. I moved my family here during the summer of 2013.

Life on the farm is certainly different than what I've known for the last thirty-one years living in the South Florida suburbs. This morning, I found myself caring for a goat named Iris who had scabs on her udder, which necessitated me bottle-feeding her twin boys Jack and Jake. I also tossed organic feed to our chickens, sheep, and cattle. We have created a small homestead farm within our larger ranch, which is spread out on 4,000 acres of rolling hills in the Ozarks.

We're working on a soil-building project, using wood chips composted with manure. It's our hope in the next several years that the acres we've covered with six to twelve inches of this dark brown and pungent-smelling material will provide some of the best soil in the world. The produce we'll grow with the new topsoil, along with the growing flocks of chickens and herds of cattle, goats, and sheep, will be used to feed our family as well as families in need one day. So will the luscious organic fruit coming from a small orchard that we've planted with more than one hundred fruit trees.

When will we start sharing this bounty of God's harvest with others? I'm not sure, which begs a second question: So why did my family and I pick up stakes in the Sunshine State and move to the rural Ozarks, where the paved driveway from the main road to our modest 1970s-era, 1,300 square-foot cabin is three miles long? Because I believe God has spoken to me—just as He spoke to Joseph in a dream more than 3,500 years ago.

I'll share what I heard from the Lord in a moment, but from a historical perspective, as I look around, it would appear that things are moving forward with our economy and our educational, medical, and agricultural systems. Technology is booming, and industry and population continues to expand. While there are way too many hurting families, on the whole most everyone has enough to eat, a roof over their heads, and speedy transportation—the trappings of civilized society that has benefited from unprecedented technological progress in my lifetime.

Despite upbeat economic and societal indicators, I believe there will come a time where this period of plenty will be followed by famine and drought, starvation, peril, and pestilence—just like in the days of Joseph. You see, I've had this dream—two, actually—and I believe that God is raising up myself and thousands of others to be Josephs to this generation.

My first dream—or vision, if you will—dates back to 2008, sometime in the spring. I was riding in the back of a forty-five-foot bus painted red, white, and blue with the logos from a book I wrote called *Perfect Weight America*. It felt pretty cool riding on a converted tour bus for music artists. In fact, we were told our Prevost bus was used by James Taylor's band when they were out touring the previous year. I like James Taylor's music quite a bit, "Carolina in My Mind" probably being my favorite song of his.

I was on the road in the midst of a yearlong tour to promote *Perfect Weight America*, eager to share my message of healthy eating, nutritional supplementation, emotional health, and functional fitness during a coast-to-coast adventure across the United States. I planned to present seminars at local health food stores, schools, and universities, visit farms, conduct interviews with the media, and film episodes for my cable TV show, *Perfect Weight America*. A camera crew was on hand to follow me everywhere. This was like living in a reality show.

Each time we passed a large ranch or farm, however, I was disappointed by what I saw. Everywhere I looked, I viewed huge machinery, the applications of chemical fertilizers, pesticides, herbicides, and fungicides, and overcrowded feedlots. American agriculture had become mechanized "agribusiness."

The picture was a different story when I visited small farms in search of healthy dairy and meat products. While these devoted farmers had all the right intentions, I noticed how a lack of resources kept many of these small farmers from producing foods and beverages of the highest quality and safety.

And then one day, while the tour bus rolled along miles and miles of asphalt through the Midwest, I looked out at the massive expanse of cropland. My eyes were attracted to the green fields streaming past my window. The idea of farming and getting back to my roots appealed to me, as I think it appeals to most people. It's in our roots, if you will.

At one time, the question wasn't, *Did your family farm?* It was, *Where did your family farm and raise food?* The reason I say this is because there's a solid chance that your great-grandparents lived an agrarian lifestyle. As recently as 1920, less than one hundred years ago, there were 6.5 million farms in the United States, home to roughly 32 million Americans, or 30 percent of the U.S. population. Today, the situation is far different. Just 2.2 million farms—or one-third of yesteryear—dot American's rural landscape. Farm and ranch families comprise just 2 percent of the U.S. population.

Large-scale farming involving massive mechanized equipment and heavy use of pesticides and chemical fertilizers has become the norm. The latest trend is the rise of genetically modified (GMO) crops, which are created by taking genes from one organism and inserting them into another to make them grow higher, larger, denser, and more resistant to insect infestation.

As we motored past verdant fields, the sight of genetically modified mono-crop agriculture stared me in the face. I didn't see a beautiful landscape anymore. I saw my children's and eventual grandchildren's stolen future. I saw a decimated countryside and a broken-down food-producing system. What appeared to be good from afar was far from good. It was then that I felt the voice of the Lord speak clearly to me with words I'll never forget.

Jordan, you need to be a Joseph.

Joseph? What did He mean by that?

I decided to reread the story of Joseph in the last thirteen chapters of Genesis, the first book of the Bible. Perhaps the Lord would show me something beyond the general story of Joseph, which I knew well. (If you're not familiar with Joseph in the Bible, my co-author, Dr. Pete Sulack, and I recap his amazing story in the next chapter.) This time when I finished reading about Joseph and all the hardships he went through, the thing that struck me was how it all started with a dream.

God has used dreams as a way of communicating with His people in the past and continues to do so today. In fact, it's my belief, as well as Dr. Pete's, that everyone has a dream from God deep inside. Not necessarily a dream that requires REM sleep, but a deep-down knowing, an inspiration to be a part of something great. It's our conviction that you can change the world with *your* God-given dream. This is the essence of the "Joseph Blessing."

God has planted a dream inside of you. Dig deep into your heart of hearts and listen to His still, small voice to find your dream and realize your destiny. If you will grab a hold of that dream and find your place in God's master plan, you will receive and walk in the Joseph Blessing.

This would be a good moment to introduce my writing colleague, Dr. Pete Sulack, a chiropractor and evangelist from Knoxville, Tennessee. Four years before I rode the Perfect Weight America bus across America in 2008, God spoke to Dr. Pete in a vision that profoundly changed his life. He'll describe the revelation he received from the Lord in Chapter 4.

Dr. Pete and I became acquainted in 2012 through a mutual friend, Dr. Josh Axe, an author, radio host, and also a chiropractor from Nashville, Tennessee. Dr. Josh thought I should get to know Dr. Pete because of our common desire to impact others for Christ.

After speaking on the phone in early 2012, Dr. Pete and I agreed that we had to meet in person. Six months later, he and his wife, Stephanie, were passing through Palm Beach County after attending a Bible conference in the area. With them were their four sons, thirteen and under. While their boys and our three children played outside, we got acquainted.

Dr. Pete told me that years earlier he had seen me being interviewed on a Christian TV show about my book, *The Maker's Diet*. This would have been around 2005. At the time, Dr. Pete had started his chiropractic practice in Knoxville and seen God bless his work. As he watched me on TV that evening, he felt the Lord say this to him in his spirit: *Someday, you and Jordan are going to work together.*

We remained in touch, and not long after we met, Dr. Pete and I started working together, teaching doctors and patients the principles of healthy living. Recently, Dr. Pete suggested we work together on a book idea called *The Joseph Blessing*.

When we met and talked about the message we wanted to share, it was great discovering that we had similar Joseph-like dreams as well as identical thoughts for inspiring others with *The Joseph Blessing*.

So here's the game plan. Over the next few chapters, we'll retell the Joseph story and then I'll share a second dream I had. Next, Dr. Pete will describe his supernatural experience with the Lord, and then we'll outline the seven steps that will help you walk in the Joseph Blessing all the days of your life.

May your God-given dream begin to change the world today!

2

THE AMAZING
TECHNICOLOR
STORY OF JOSEPH

THE NARRATIVE OF JOSEPH, A DREAM-INTERPRETING SHEP-
herd who was sold into slavery but eventually rose from the
depths of prison to become the prime minister of the most
powerful nation in the civilized world, is one of the more lay-
ered and elaborate stories found in the Old Testament.

Joseph saved Egypt. Joseph also saved the nation of his
family, the children of his father, Israel.

Many today are aware of the story of Joseph through a
long-ago Sunday school class or a high school rendition of
the Andrew Lloyd Webber musical, *Joseph and the Amazing
Technicolor Dreamcoat*, which has been staged nearly 25,000

times by amateur theater groups since it was first performed in London in 1970.

I (Jordan) was a teen when I watched a longhaired Donny Osmond play the lead role of the film version of *Joseph and the Amazing Technicolor Dreamcoat*. Unfortunately, the zany production reduced Joseph to a caricature of a go-with-the-flow wayfarer decked out in a psychedelic "dreamcoat" right out of the sixties. I believe the Joseph story deserves far better than a well-rehearsed musical portrayal by Donny Osmond.

Joseph's life is a testament to how you can remain true to God regardless of what life throws at you. He exhibited godly character and great faithfulness in times of trial. Joseph demonstrated his integrity and forthrightness when interacting with others. And he showed mercy to undeserving brothers who sold him into slavery.

The Joseph described in Genesis really existed, and that's an idea worth keeping in mind. It's easy to forget that ancient stories in the Bible—especially in the Old Testament—involved real people, living real lives in a real world. Joseph's story began in the land of Canaan, known today as Palestine, Syria, and Israel, sometime around 1600 to 1700 B.C.

Joseph was born the eleventh of twelve sons to a wealthy nomad named Jacob and his beloved wife, Rachel. We're not told exactly why, but Joseph was clearly the apple of his father's eye, the favorite among all his sons. Perhaps the favoritism stemmed from the fact that, at the time, Joseph was the only child born of Rachel, whom Jacob loved dearly from the moment he laid eyes on her.

We know that Joseph wasn't afraid to speak up as a young man. He "brought a bad report" about his half-brothers—the sons of Leah, Bilhah, and Zilpah, his father's other wives—directly to Jacob (Genesis 37:2). His tattle-telling didn't endear him to his bros.

Sibling rivalry was even more acute in ancient cultures when polygamous marriages were commonplace. Because children were born by different wives, each mother wanted the best for her offspring—especially when their sons stood in line for their share of the inheritance. Joseph and later a younger brother named Benjamin were born of Rachel, while the remaining ten sons of Jacob came from other mothers.

Jacob overtly displayed his favoritism of Joseph when he made him a tunic or coat "of many colors." This, too, is a significant part of Joseph's story. More than three thousand years ago, you didn't drive to the local department store and shop the aisles for a colorful coat or robe; you had to weave it yourself. Dyes were a precious commodity in the ancient world. Eye-popping colors like red and purple were held in high esteem, and the color purple signified royalty. A tunic or coat of red and purple would have reinforced Jacob's message that Joseph was more special than the others. Genesis 37:4 (NKJV) says, "But when his brothers saw that their father loved him more than all his brothers, they hated him and could not speak peaceably to him."

Joseph was seventeen years old when he received his "Technicolor dreamcoat." After his brothers gave him the cold shoulder, Scripture tells us what happened next:

Now Joseph had a dream, and he told it to his brothers; and they hated him even more. So he said to them, "Please hear this dream which I have dreamed: There we were, binding sheaves in the field. Then behold, my sheaf arose and also stood upright; and indeed your sheaves stood all around and bowed down to my sheaf."

And his brothers said to him, "Shall you indeed reign over us? Or shall you have dominion over us?" So they hated him even more for his dreams and for his words (Genesis 37:5-8).

We can only imagine that dinner-time conversations within Jacob's clan got a little testy after Joseph informed his brothers that one day they would bow to him in honor.

Then Joseph doubled down and told his family about a *second* dream similar to the first. In this vision, the sun, the moon, and eleven stars were bowing down to him. The inference was crystal clear to everyone: the sun was his father, the moon was his mother, and the eleven stars were his brothers. This dream was even over the top for Joseph's doting dad.

His father [Jacob] *rebuked him and said to him, "What is this dream that you have dreamed? Shall your mother and I and your brothers indeed come to bow down to the earth before you?" And his brothers envied him, but his father kept the matter in mind* (Genesis 37:10-11).

His brothers conspired to kill Joseph, talking among themselves about showing their brother who was boss. When Jacob asked Joseph to check up on his brothers pasturing their flocks at Dothan, little did Joseph know that he was walking into a trap.

> *Then they said to one another, "Look, this dreamer is coming! Come therefore, let us now kill him and cast him into some pit; and we shall say, 'Some wild beast has devoured him.' We shall see what will become of his dreams!"* (Genesis 37:19-20).

It fell upon the oldest son, Reuben, to talk reason into his roughneck brothers. After all, they were talking about murdering their own flesh and blood. He counseled them not to kill Joseph outright but to throw him into a pit and leave him there to die. Reuben had an ulterior motive, though, which was to come back later, rescue Joseph, and return him safe and sound to his father.

Joseph's conspiring brothers agreed to Reuben's plan. They swarmed Joseph, mercilessly beat him, and stripped him of his famous coat. Then they tossed him into a deep, empty pit with no food or water to sustain him.

All that drama made the brothers hungry because Scripture says the next thing they did was sit down for a meal. They were still feasting when a caravan of camels bearing spices, balm, and myrrh passed by, meandering in a southerly direction for Egypt. They were Ishmaelite traders who were descendants of Midian.

Judah, the fourth son of Jacob and full brother of Reuben, had an idea: *Why don't we kill two birds with one stone? We'll sell Joseph to the Ishmaelite traders, and that way we won't have blood on our hands. We'll never see him again, and we'll make a little money as well. Problem solved.*

Scripture tells us that Reuben didn't know his brothers brokered a deal to sell Joseph into slavery for twenty pieces of silver; he must have been tending to the flocks when the exchange was made. It's likely that the teenage Joseph did not go easily when he learned of his brothers' betrayal. Fight as he might, ropes and whips moved him in the direction of Egypt with the Ishmaelite traders.

When Reuben returned to the pit to check on Joseph, his younger brother was gone. After discovering the truth from his brothers, Reuben ripped his own tunic in half down to his belly button—a sign of grief in Old Testament times—and asked his guilty siblings how they were going to explain what happened back home.

The brothers came up with a plan: sprinkle Joseph's colorful coat with plenty of goat's blood and present the stained garment as proof that Joseph had met an untimely fate in the wilderness.

Their ruse worked. Jacob was convinced that a wild beast had ripped his son to pieces. The patriarch tore his clothes, wrapped sackcloth around his waist, and mourned his son for many days. All his sons and daughters attempted to comfort him, but Jacob could not be consoled. The loss was too great.

FLIGHT INTO EGYPT

Joseph's owners sold him in Egypt to Potiphar, an officer of Pharaoh and captain of the guard. Because of his high position, Potiphar wielded power—or at least knew where the levers of power existed.

After such a rotten break in life, Joseph's devotion to God did not bend one iota, however:

> *The Lord was with Joseph, and he was a successful man; and he was in the house of his master the Egyptian. And his master saw that the Lord was with him and that the Lord made all he did to prosper in his hand. So Joseph found favor in his sight, and served him. Then he made him overseer of his house, and all that he had he put under his authority.*
>
> *So it was, from the time that he had made him overseer of his house and all that he had, that the Lord blessed the Egyptian's house for Joseph's sake; and the blessing of the Lord was on all that he had in the house and in the field. Thus he left all that he had in Joseph's hand, and he did not know what he had except for the bread which he ate.*
>
> *Now Joseph was handsome in form and appearance* (Genesis 39:2-6).

The last sentence looks like an add-on thought, but it's telling. Joseph, late in his teens, was at the height of his physical powers. He was good looking. Carried himself well, was confident and sure of himself, and had learned a new language or two. He obviously had made lemonade out of lemons.

Just as he was forging an identity in a new land, Potiphar's wife pulled a Mrs. Robinson. "Lie with me," she said, employing a euphemism understood by both parties. His answer covered all the bases:

> Look, my master does not know what is with me in the house, and he has committed all that he has to my hand. There is no one greater in this house than I, nor has he kept back anything from me but you, because you are his wife. How then can I do this great wickedness, and sin against God? (Genesis 39:8b-9)

Potiphar's wife, who is not named, didn't get mad at being turned down. She got even. The next time she and Joseph were alone in the house, she propositioned him again. When he repeated an emphatic *no* and attempted to flee, she grabbed his cloak and ripped off a piece. Holding part of his tunic gave her an idea—a horrible idea.

She showed the piece of garment to her husband and described a false story about Joseph attempting to rape her, but her screams prevented the attack. When Joseph took off, she grabbed at his cloak, which is why she was in possession of a piece of his garment.

In a she-said, he-said dispute between Potiphar's wife and a house slave, guess who won? Joseph was dumped into the king's prison, and the key was thrown away. Once again, Joseph stayed in character and refused to change who he was. He rolled with another huge setback, as this section of Scripture states:

> *But the Lord was with Joseph in the prison and showed him his faithful love. And the Lord made Joseph a favorite with the prison warden. Before long, the warden put Joseph in charge of all the other prisoners and over everything that happened in prison. The warden had no more worries, because Joseph took care of everything. The Lord was with him and caused everything he did to succeed* (Genesis 39:21-23 NLT).

Why should we be surprised? Clearly, God had blessed Joseph with amazing administrative gifts, but that wasn't enough to earn him a get-out-of-jail-free card. He remained behind bars.

THE CUP BEARER AND THE BAKER

Some time later—probably five to ten years—Pharaoh's chief cup-bearer and chief baker either said something they shouldn't have to the king, or they crossed him. We're not told why in Genesis, but after the cup bearer and baker "offended" the king of Egypt, they were tossed into prison alongside Joseph.

A cup bearer was an important position in ancient times. He was an officer of high rank in royal courts who did more than pour wine during feasts and meal times. A cup bearer had to be totally trustworthy because it was his responsibility to make sure no one poisoned Pharaoh's wine. Sometimes he was required to drink from Pharaoh's cup *before* he sipped—just to be sure the cup of wine wasn't spiked with poison hemlock.

Under such circumstances, Pharaoh and his cup bearer formed a close personal bond—one looking out for the other. The cup bearer also kept his ear to the ground because of the constant fear of plots and threats against Pharaoh.

The chief baker was another close aide to Pharaoh. He had to be perceived as trustworthy because he was responsible for much of the food served at the royal table.

After Pharaoh's cup bearer and baker fell out of favor and landed in prison, they each had a dream that neither could interpret. The jailhouse scuttlebutt was that Joseph could interpret dreams, so the cup bearer approached him and described his vision:

> *Behold, in my dream a vine was before me, and in the vine were three branches; it was as though it budded, its blossoms shot forth, and its clusters brought forth ripe grapes. Then Pharaoh's cup was in my hand; and I took the grapes and pressed them into Pharaoh's cup, and placed the cup in Pharaoh's hand* (Genesis 40:9b-11).

Joseph said, "Here's my interpretation," and it was good news. Within three days, the cup bearer would be restored to his former position, and everything would be like it was before. When that happened, Joseph asked the cup bearer to "please show kindness to me; make mention to me to Pharaoh, and get me out of this house" (Genesis 40:14b).

Hearing about Joseph's interpretation and how well it turned out for the cup bearer, the chief baker implored Joseph to interpret his dream as well. This time, Joseph's interpretation wasn't as upbeat. He said something would also happen in three days, but it would be calamitous for the chief baker. He would be hanged, and his body would be pecked by birds eating his flesh.

And that's exactly what happened.

Three days later, the cup bearer was back in Pharaoh's good graces and the baker was vulture food. So did the cup bearer put in a good word for Joseph? *Nooooo.* He forgot about him and allowed Joseph to continue to rot in prison.

A TIME OF PLENTY, A TIME OF FAMINE

Two more long years ensued, at which time Pharaoh had a pair of dreams—scary dreams. In the first, seven fat, healthy cows were munching on lush grass on a riverbank when seven ugly and gaunt cows came out of the water and devoured the plump, happy cows. In the second dream, seven ears of full-bodied grain grew out of a single stalk. Then seven more ears grew up, but they were thin and dried out by the east wind. The thin ears, however, swallowed up the seven heads of healthy grain.

The dreams were so real that Pharaoh was greatly troubled—and asked for help about what they meant. His closest advisors as well as his magicians and sages were stumped. No one could come up with a plausible explanation for the meaning of Pharaoh's dreams.

Then the cup bearer suddenly remembered—Joseph could interpret dreams! *Well, Pharaoh, it goes like this. There's this guy, a Hebrew slave actually, that I met when you threw me and the chief baker into prison. While we were there, the chief baker and I had mysterious dreams that defied explanation, but Joseph interpreted them perfectly. Within three days, I was returned to my station in your court, but the chief baker was hanged—just as Joseph predicted.*

That was enough for Pharaoh to demand that Joseph be brought before him—immediately. The next thing Joseph knew, he was shaving off his beard, changing into fresh clothing, and being ushered into Pharaoh's presence at the palace. Twelve years had passed since his brothers shanghaied him into slavery.

"I had dreams last night, but no one here can tell me what they mean," Pharaoh said. "But I've heard it said of you that you can understand and interpret dreams."

Joseph's answer was classic: "It is beyond my power to do this, but God can. He will tell me what your dreams mean."

Joseph listened to Pharaoh describe both dreams. He didn't hesitate to relate his explanation:

"Your two dreams mean the same thing," he began. "God is telling you that the seven healthy cows and the seven healthy ears of grain represent seven years of bumper crops, but the seven sick and ugly cows and the seven scrawny ears of grain represent seven years of famine. What God is trying to tell you is that seven years of plenty are on their way throughout Egypt, but after that there will be seven years where there will be nothing to eat in the land."

"So what should I do?" Pharaoh asked.

"You need to appoint a wise and experienced man and put him in charge of Egypt so that he can stockpile plenty of grain during the years ahead. Then the country won't be devastated by the coming famine."

Pharaoh spread out his palms. "Who can take on this task?" he asked rhetorically. No one volunteered. Then Pharaoh had an idea.

"Wait a minute. God has given you special insight, Joseph, so I'm appointing you in charge of all of Egypt. All my people will report to you. Only I will be over you."

Pharaoh sealed the deal by taking his signet ring from his finger and slipping it on one of Joseph's fingers. Then he outfitted him in robes of the best linen and put a gold chain around his neck. Pharaoh even gave him a sweet ride—a chariot at his disposal.

Joseph was thirty years old when he assumed his duties—similar to what a prime minster is today—over the land of

Egypt. Just as he predicted, the next seven years produced bumper crops. Joseph made sure that the surplus was stored in barns within Egypt's major cities and towns. During this time, he married Asenath, the Egyptian daughter of Potiphera. Their union produced two sons.

Seven years later, famine arrived with a vengeance. Egypt was ready because Joseph had stockpiled so much grain that he had trouble keeping track of it all. The rest of the world wasn't prepared for devastating food shortages. As crops withered from drought, the whole world made a beeline for Egypt in search of grain so they wouldn't starve to death.

The famine was unprecedented. No one outside of Egypt was unaffected, including Jacob, his eleven sons, and their families living in Canaan. When Jacob learned there was food in Egypt, he said to his sons, "Why don't you travel to Egypt and buy food before we starve to death?"

Desperate and driven by hunger, ten of Joseph's brothers caravanned to Egypt, but Jacob requested that Benjamin stay behind because he had a feeling that something bad would happen to him.

The sons weren't alone on the dirt paths snaking their way south. The travel route was packed with camels and other animals led by teams eager to buy Egyptian grain. These desperate times called for desperate measures.

Joseph called the shots on the grain sales; everything had to be run through him because his central authority managed the storehouses. When Joseph's brothers arrived in Egypt—we're not told where exactly—they were led into his presence, most likely at Pharaoh's palace, an imposing edifice that bespoke power and supremacy.

Joseph's brothers requested an audience. When they walked in, they bowed, as people in their position would do. Thus, Joseph's long-ago prediction that his brothers would bow before him became true.

Joseph immediately recognized them, and we can only imagine the jolt his nervous system received. His brothers didn't know who he was. After all, it had been a good twenty years since they sold him off to the Ishmaelite traders. After being raised up by Pharaoh and presiding over seven years of plenty, Joseph was in his late thirties, mature in every way. Perhaps Joseph's head was shaved and he wore black eyeliner as well as gilded robes befitting a minister from Pharaoh's court. Then again, it would be inconceivable to Jacob's sons that the brother they sold into slavery was now the second most important man in the world.

Joseph maintained his composure, but he spoke roughly, demanding, "Where do you come from?" He conversed in the local language and used an interpreter.

"From Canaan," one of the brothers replied. "We've come to buy food."

"No, you haven't. You're spies. You've come this far to look for ways you can attack Egypt."

"Oh, no, that's not true!" one of the brothers declared. "We're all sons of the same man. We're honest people. We'd never think about spying."

"No, you're spies. You're looking for our weak spots."

The brothers tried to explain that they were twelve sons of the same man in Canaan. The youngest was back home with the father, and the other one was no more.

Joseph's heart had to break in half upon hearing that admission. Nonetheless, he maintained a poker face and acted unconvinced that this band of brothers from Canaan was on the up and up.

"Here's what we're going to do," he said, as he laid out a test. If what they were saying was true, then they were to send one of the brothers back home and bring back the missing brother. But first, he ordered that all of them be thrown into prison to show that he meant business. "We'll see if you've been telling the truth or not," he said, "but as Pharaoh lives, I say you're spies."

After three days in jail, Joseph brought his brothers back before him. He announced that he had changed his mind. Declaring that he was a God-fearing man, he had decided that one of the brothers would stay behind in prison while the others took back food and then returned with the other brother. "Do that, and not one of you will die," Joseph promised.

The terrified brothers talked among themselves. This was not what they expected when they set off for Egypt. One said it was payback for what they did to Joseph years earlier. "We saw how terrified he was when he was begging us for mercy," one brother said. "And now we're paying for his murder."

The brothers didn't know that Joseph understood every word. He stepped away for a moment and had a good cry, then composed himself. When he returned, his brothers still had no idea what was happening. All they knew was this Egyptian minister held all the cards.

Joseph ordered that Simeon be tied up and taken prisoner. Then he commanded that all their sacks be filled with grain before they were sent on their way. He accepted their payment of coins.

After the brothers had left his presence, he directed his steward to stuff their money back into their bags of grain.

We can only imagine the traumatic reaction of Jacob when the brothers returned to Canaan, short one brother. After the remaining ten brothers described what happened in Egypt, the patriarch nearly keeled over after being told that Simeon was a hostage *and* the Egyptian minister had demanded that Benjamin accompany his brothers when they returned.

Or else.

These developments were almost more than Jacob could bear. Then the brothers discovered that their purses of money were inside the bags of grain!

How did their money get there? What were they thinking back in Egypt? Surely, the Egyptians had discovered their money was missing. Further complicating their lives was the minister's insistence that they return to Egypt with Benjamin or face the loss of Simeon to the slave traders. Yet Jacob declared that he would not allow Benjamin to travel to Egypt. The patriarch maintained that losing his youngest son would send him to the grave.

THE RETURN TRIP

The famine continued, and it didn't take Jacob and his clan long to consume the food they brought back with them from Egypt. As their supplies dwindled, it was apparent to everyone that the brothers would have to return to Egypt to purchase more grain. This was problematic, however. The brothers reminded their father that they wouldn't even be given an audience with the Egyptian minister if they failed to appear without their youngest brother.

Jacob moaned but he didn't relent—until they were on the verge of starvation. He gave in, saying, "If it has to be, then it has to be." But he told his sons to take along gifts of balm and honey, as well as spices and perfume—and double the money—so they could get on the good side of the Egyptian prime minister. And off the brothers went, with Benjamin in tow.

Upon their arrival, Joseph did something unexpected. He pulled his steward aside and told him to take his brothers to his personal residence, kill a fatted calf, and prepare a huge feast. Then Joseph excused himself and departed without saying a word.

The brothers wondered if they had walked into another trap. When the steward explained the new plan, their anxiety levels shot through the roof. The Egyptian surely knew about the money in the bags, and this was a trap to enslave them. They would never see Canaan again.

They warily followed the steward to Joseph's opulent house, as befitting the second most powerful man in Egypt. The brothers figured their best chance was to come clean. Along the way, they told the steward about how their purses of money were found in their bags of grain after they arrived in Canaan.

The steward waved off their concerns. "Everything's in order," he said. "Don't worry about a thing. Your God and the God of your father must have given you a bonus. I was paid in full."

The brothers looked at each other in amazement. Another surprise came when Simeon was reunited with his brothers. They were quickly ushered into the main salon, where their hands and feet were washed.

At noontime, Joseph showed up. The brothers presented their gifts of honey and spices and then bowed respectfully before him.

Once again, his brothers bowed low to him, just as his dreams predicted.

Joseph made small talk about the famine, and then asked how their father was. Was he well?

"Oh, yes, your servant, our father, is doing quite well," responded one of his brothers.

Joseph's eyes looked around until he spotted Benjamin. "Is this your youngest brother you told me about?" he inquired.

Joseph didn't wait for answer. He excused himself and hurried to another room, where he was overcome with emotion. After another good cry, he composed himself, washed his face, and returned for the midday meal.

He did not sit with his guests, as protocol demanded. Egyptians looked down upon foreigners, especially the Hebrew people. Joseph made sure plenty of meat and other delicious foods made it to his brothers' table and ordered that Benjamin receive a double portion. Wine flowed.

When the feast was over, Joseph pulled his faithful steward close and gave him specific instructions to fill everyone's bags with grain—as much as they could carry. But Joseph added a twist: the steward was ordered to put his personal silver chalice inside of Benjamin's bag.

The following morning at the break of dawn, Jacob's sons began the long trek home. Imagine the looks of surprise—and terror—on their faces when they noticed Joseph's steward chasing after them on his horse. Several soldiers were with him. When the troupe caught up with them, the steward said Joseph's prized chalice was missing. Had one of them taken it?

The brothers indignantly swore that none of them would do such an evil act, especially to someone who had saved their clan from starving. One of the brothers said, "Search us. If the chalice is found among us, that person will die and the rest of us will become your slaves."

"You don't have to go that far," the steward said. "But if someone is found with my master's chalice, then he will become my slave. The rest of you will be allowed to return to your home."

The steward searched the bags, from the oldest to the youngest. Of course, he knew the magnificent cup was in one of Benjamin's bags. The steward had placed it there.

Upon the discovery of the missing chalice, the brothers tore their clothes in despair. They had no choice but to return to the palace grounds with the steward.

Imagine the scene upon their arrival. Joseph angrily demanding an explanation. The brothers standing accused, looking at their sandals. Judah taking the role of family spokesman and saying, "How can we prove our innocence? We're all in this together, so we're ready to be your slaves."

Joseph calmly replied that wouldn't be necessary. Only Benjamin had to stay behind. The rest were free to leave.

Judah said that wouldn't work.

"Why's that?" Joseph asked.

"Because our father couldn't bear the loss of his youngest son after his brother, born of the same mother, turned up missing years ago. His grief would send him to the grave," Judah reported.

Here's what happened next, according to Scripture:

Then Joseph could not restrain himself before all those who stood by him, and he cried out, "Make everyone go out from me!" So no one stood with him while Joseph made himself known to his brothers. And he wept aloud, and the Egyptians and the house of Pharaoh heard it.

Then Joseph said to his brothers, "I am Joseph; does my father still live?" But his brothers could not answer him, for they were dismayed in his presence. And Joseph said to his brothers, "Please come near to me." So they came near. Then he said: "I am Joseph your brother, whom you sold into Egypt. But now, do not therefore be grieved or angry with yourselves because you sold me here; for God sent me before you to preserve life. For these two years the famine has been in the land, and there are still five years in which there will be neither plowing nor harvesting. And God sent me before you to preserve a posterity for you in the earth, and to save your lives by a great deliverance. So now it was not you who sent me here, but God; and He has made me a father to Pharaoh, and lord of all his house, and a ruler throughout all the land of Egypt" (Genesis 45:1-8).

Joseph then outlined a plan. The brothers would return to their father, tell him the good news, and then pack up immediately and move to Goshen, a part of Egypt. They would be close to Joseph so that he could keep an eye on them—and make sure they had enough provisions. He reiterated his promise to have his family resettled on the best land in Egypt. "You will live off the fat of the land," he promised. Pharaoh was on board with Joseph's plan.

Seventy members of Jacob's family picked up stakes and moved to Goshen, including their patriarch. Joseph was waiting for them when they arrived. His reunion with his father, old and nearing the end of his life, packed more emotional punch than a dozen Hallmark movies.

And that's how the nation of Israel—God's chosen name for Jacob—came to be. And Scripture tells us that Jacob and his descendants "grew and multiplied exceedingly" (Genesis 47:27).

After all that Joseph had been through, God had greatly blessed and used him to bring physical and spiritual salvation, first to his family and then to the rest of the world. What started with a young boy's dream led to the very salvation of the known world.

BRINGING IT FULL CIRCLE

When I read the Genesis account while on the Perfect Weight America tour, I realized that Joseph wasn't just a dreamer who got himself into a pickle. He was someone who was close to the Lord in thought and in actions. I was impressed by the amount of wisdom God gave Joseph to store up food during seven years of plenty.

And now, on a tour bus, the Lord was telling me to be a Joseph.

What was that going to look like?

3

THROWN INTO THE PIT

WHEN PHARAOH'S ADVISORS HEARD JOSEPH'S INTERPRETA-
tion of Pharaoh's dreams, they thought the former prisoner
was nuts. Joseph, however, had street cred because he had
correctly interpreted the dreams of the cup bearer and baker.
Ultimately, Joseph was proven right.

It's mind-boggling, when you stop and think about it,
how Joseph came out of a deep pit and was elevated to the
highest heights within the greatest kingdom and civilization in the world. On top of that, Joseph was used by God
as an instrument to save and redeem Jacob's family, which
became the twelve tribes of Israel. The Messiah would be
born through this very lineage, which is an awesome thought.

Like I (Jordan) said earlier, when the Lord spoke to me
and said I would become a Joseph, I wasn't sure what that

meant. I continued to read my Bible, asking God to speak to me through His Word.

There was precedence in my life for taking this approach. Years earlier, when I was diagnosed with multiple incurable diseases, I had scoured the Scriptures to determine what God's plan was for health, healing, and eating. I received incredible revelation that led me to write *The Maker's Diet*, which became a *New York Times* bestseller, as well as nearly two dozen books on the topics of health and wellness.

This time, I was on a search for God's definition of stewardship and biblical wealth. I learned that Abraham grew wealthy with cattle, gold, and silver. That Isaac planted a field and reaped a hundredfold harvest. That Jacob grew his flocks and his herds with wisdom and discernment...at least until famine ravaged the land. And finally I read that Job was blessed "twice as much" later in life with sheep, camels, and donkeys.

When Almighty God, through the psalmist, described His wealth in Psalms 50:10 as owning the cattle on a thousand hills, it dawned on me that I should probably own the cattle on one or two hills myself. I immediately began to pray about investing in something that God called value, or what we generally describe today as hard assets.

Propelling me was a deep desire to care for my family and those close to me. I had been married to Nicki for nearly ten years, and together we were raising three children (including two recently adopted infants). We discussed how the Lord was asking me to become a Joseph and what that looked like in today's world.

Consider the context. Remember, this conversation between Nicki and me happened in the spring of 2008, a time when this country was in the throes of the "Great Recession." Seemingly overnight, investments and portfolios shrunk greatly in value. Trillions of dollars of assets were wiped out. Some lost everything they had.

But what was this "money" anyway? A bunch of pixelized numbers on a computer screen. Commerce happened whenever someone slid a plastic card through a reader or went online and typed in sixteen numbers, an expiration date, a security code, and clicked Order Now.

I struggled with the fact that my assets were a bunch of numbers in the ether, linked in cyberspace by coaxial cables to central banks. For the small amount of real money in my wallet, what was behind my cash anyway? Nothing tangible as far as I saw. My Andrew Jacksons and George Washingtons were backed by a promise from the U.S. Treasury that they were worth something—an IOU if you will. U.S. currency stopped being backed by gold in the 1970s.

I was enough of a student to know that those who ignore history are doomed to repeat it—and that life has a way of skittering in directions that you'd never think possible when you're living right in the midst of it.

I first absorbed this lesson when I heard the backstory of my grandmother, Rose, who grew up in a quaint Polish village in the 1920s. She was a young girl when the new German chancellor, Adolf Hitler, began making life very difficult for Jewish people like her. Hitler's actions sparked the rise of anti-Semitism throughout Europe.

Rose and her family witnessed the escalation in tension against God's chosen people. Fortunately for them, they got out in time. My grandmother was thirteen when she and her parents, plus four siblings, immigrated to the United States in 1935. Two older sisters, Sonya and Dora, elected to stay behind, however, because they were married with their own families. Their husbands had jobs, and their children were in school. They believed their government and army would protect them from Nazi aggression, if the threat was in fact a reality, which they were not sure of at the time.

We know how that turned out for the Jewish people. In Sonya and Dora's situation, they were rounded up by the SS during the *blitzkrieg* invasion in 1939 and paraded through the streets along with other Jewish families. Then the children were separated from their parents and shot while mothers and fathers screamed. Next, the women were ordered to gather, and they were gunned down in full view of their husbands. And finally the men stood shoulder to shoulder in front of the machine guns. Entire families were massacred in minutes.

The amazing part of the story is that this happened less than eighty years ago, not one thousand years ago. It seems inconceivable that mass murder would materialize in this country, but it's not inconceivable that our economy could collapse. If the latter were to happen, and it's my prayer that it never will, gold and silver won't be enough. You can't eat gold and you can't hydrate yourself with silver. Nor can you protect yourself with bronze or clothe yourself with platinum. The only things valuable are foods you can eat, beverages you can drink, clothes you can wear, and roofs over your head. The same things that were valuable thousands of years ago are the *only* true items of value today.

It was at this point that I realized I needed to be able to produce food and provide places of refuge for people in need when times got tough. I didn't want to rely on grocery stores for my family's food. These days, the average supermarket has enough foodstuffs on hand for four days—and just sixteen hours in small grocery stores in Manhattan, for example. Living many years in Florida reminded me of how store shelves could be stripped bare in an afternoon when the Weather Channel announced the imminent arrival of a major hurricane.

I took ownership of my dream to become a Joseph. During the *Perfect Weight America* bus tour, I starting looking at pieces of land where I could grow crops, raise livestock, produce meat, have a dairy operation, and tap into sustainable sources of water.

I truly believed that God was raising up men and women like me to become Josephs to take care of the physical needs of people. What better way to share the message of Jesus? I imagined what it would be like extending the hands of God to children and widows and watching their family members light up and ask, "Why are you doing this?"

At the same time, I knew my dream of buying property and raising cattle and crops sounded preposterous to some of my friends and acquaintances. I was a suburb slicker from the east coast of Florida used to a comfortable life inside a gated community. I wore dress shoes and designer jeans, not leather boots and well-worn Levis with big belt buckles. I owned two dozen baseball caps and not a single Stetson. I couldn't recall getting my hands dirty and certainly didn't have a green thumb. In fact, I'd never grown anything in my life. I really didn't know much about landscaping other than looking at the flowers and St. Augustine grass outside my home.

Then something very interesting happened after I told others about my dream of buying a ranch and a farm and the plan to store up food and water for people in need.

I was thrown into the pit, just like Joseph.

News Out of Nowhere

I got into a routine during the Perfect Weight America tour in early 2008. After a week's worth of book signings, speaking engagements, and media appearances, I would typically host a weekend health conference at a local church. Once I finished on Saturday night, I'd board a red-eye to Florida so that I could spend Sunday and Monday with my family.

Sometime in early June, I noticed a pain in my groin. It felt like a pulled muscle. Maybe it was a hernia. I was thirty-two years old and in excellent physical condition, so I knew my body well. Something didn't feel right.

After trying several methods to reduce the pain and even trying to "push through it," I decided to see a doctor.

I told him I suspected an inguinal hernia. My physician poked and prodded. At first he agreed with me, but after some discussion, he thought I may not have a hernia, which portended something more serious. He convinced me that exploratory surgery was needed to determine what was going on.

Following the procedure, I was wheeled into the lobby and was told by the doctor that I didn't have a hernia. Instead, I had cancer.

My world swirled. How could I have cancer at my age? How could I have cancer when I'd been consuming only the healthiest organic sources of meat, vegetables, and grains for most of my adult life? How could I have cancer when I had *never* cheated by eating anything with white sugar, high fructose corn syrup, conventional white flour, or genetically modified ingredients?

The irony was inescapable. Someone who'd written nineteen books on health and wellness, including *The Great Physician's Rx for Cancer*, had contracted a life-threatening disease that killed millions each year. Someone who was called upon by entertainers, pastors, and professional athletes to coach them on their health was facing a death sentence.

The doctor scheduled me for a CT scan to determine if the cancer had spread.

A few days after the scan, I returned to the doctor's office to have my staples taken out and receive the results. Nicki joined me. When my doctor came into the examination room, I'll admit to some apprehension.

I asked him what he found. He didn't beat around the bush. "There's more to discuss," the doctor informed me.

After the doctor finished taking out the staples in my abdomen, he said he'd meet us in his office to discuss the results of the scan. We walked down the hallway and stepped inside the doctor's office. I asked Nicki to stand by the door and then I got down on the floor.

I lowered my face to the ground and quoted Job 1:21 out loud: "Naked I came from my mother's womb, and naked shall I return there. The Lord gave, and the Lord has taken away; blessed be the name of the Lord."

I call this "Job's Prayer" and had quoted this passage of Scripture with my face to the ground several times in my life when circumstances were dire and I needed a miracle from God. Each time, God did for me what He did for Job by delivering me from peril and providing me with a two-fold blessing in His timing.

My doctor arrived a minute later. He looked at his notes and said I was looking at something called "radical emphatic dissection surgery" with pre- or post-op chemotherapy. Treatment had to start right away—like tomorrow.

"Could I have some time to work on this?" I asked. I wanted to search out all my options, including what I could personally do to beat back cancer with an even more radical diet and lifestyle.

"Don't mess around with this," my doctor replied sternly. "This cancer is 100 percent fatal if you don't do something quickly. It's one of the fastest-growing cancers out there."

He recommended that I go to Dana-Farber Cancer Institute/Brigham and Women's Hospital in Boston, which was a division of Harvard Medical, or to the Indiana University Simon Cancer Center, where cyclist Lance Armstrong was treated for cancer in 1996. "Go to the best of the best," my doctor said. He emphasized that if I didn't get conventional treatment, chemotherapy, and a very unpleasant surgery, there would be a 100 percent chance that I'd be dead.

I knew the dream God gave me would be tested. Instead of dealing with this life-threatening disease the way most would, I realized that this was part of His plan for my life. Against my doctor's advice, I decided to give God forty days to work a miracle. Over the course of six weeks, I committed to selling out completely and wholeheartedly to following God's plan in body, mind, and spirit.

I ceased being involved in the company I started, Garden of Life, where I was the CEO. I left the company in the capable hands of my leadership team, telling a small group of people about my situation. I spoke confidently—not that God was going to heal me, but that He already had paid the price for my sickness and I was going to walk in it.

I decided to embark on a radical diet and lifestyle program—which I will detail in an upcoming book—and continued to pray and believe for my healing. Forty days came and went, filled with faith and sometimes fear, plus much encouragement from friends and family.

After forty days in the pit, follow-up tests were conducted, and the results confounded the experts. I was cancer-free. Modern science had no explanation for why this aggressive cancer had disappeared from my body.

Relief—and gratitude—for what the Lord had done filled my body. I knew my life would never be the same. Like Joseph being released from prison, I had been released from a death sentence. This was my chance to live out the dream God gave me—a Joseph mandate, if you will.

Farmland and natural springs were purchased in southern Missouri. Livestock were procured, and seeds were gathered and planted. Infrastructure—barns and a 40,000-square-foot organic dairy-processing center—were constructed. I worked on a strategy to feed, clothe, and house people and started a new company called Beyond Organic to provide people with the world's healthiest foods and beverages.

Initially folks were excited about what we were doing as we set our sights on success. Each step of the way, I gave God the glory. I can remember looking up on a moonless night and hearing the voice of the Lord, which prompted me to say, *Look at the stars in the sky. So shall the mission marketers at Beyond Organic be.*

Beyond Organic was structured as a direct-to-consumer company where we relied on individuals—mission marketers—to share our message in order to create sales of the products. Our mission marketers were natural health practitioners, therapists, ministry leaders, homeschool moms, and passionate individuals who wanted to share our message of health and hope with those they knew and loved. The Lord was reassuring me that everything was going to be okay with Beyond Organic.

But instead of success, I was thrown into the pit *again* (or perhaps, in Joseph terms, the jail) when Beyond Organic struggled mightily from the get go.

Millions of dollars were spent and lost in a matter of months. I was moved by God to resign from my position at Garden of Life, the company I founded fifteen years earlier and which was acquired in 2009. I had remained with Garden of Life following the acquisition, but when I resigned, I walked away from a significant salary, which was very challenging considering how much money Beyond Organic was losing every month.

There were some more minor yet significant challenges as well, like the attempted trip to Florida when the luggage containing most of my clothes and personal items was stolen at the airport. Another devastating experience occurred while coaching my son Joshua's tackle football team.

Coaching football has been a passion of mine ever since I started coaching Joshua's teams in Florida. During our first fall in Missouri, coaching Joshua's new team proved to be a great escape from the challenges we were experiencing. We started the season with great success, but during our third game, my son—who happened to be the starting quarterback—fractured his arm in two places. I felt horrible for my son and what he had to go through.

A few months after we moved, we were contacted by someone who asked us if we wanted to adopt a one-year-old baby girl. When we met the baby for the first time, we were also introduced to her two older siblings—a ten-year-old girl and sixteen-year-old boy. We brought them into our home and loved them like our own children.

Less than two months later, however, their guardian decided to take them back to where they came from, ripping them out of our home. Upon hearing the news that they were leaving, the ten-year-old girl looked at me with tear-filled eyes and said, "Daddy, when I'm older, can I come find you?"

What a heartbreak. Then more sadness and sorrow happened when a good friend diagnosed with leukemia, who was actually doing very well, died unexpectedly. I held his hand while he took his last breath. What was even more devastating was the fact that his wife, Sara, was due any day with their first child.

When we moved out to Missouri, we hired a teacher to educate our children. Months later, she left us on little notice and relocated to another state, leaving Nicki to homeschool our children. And wouldn't you know it, our move from sunny South Florida to southern Missouri was welcomed with the worst winter in nearly one hundred years with five big snow storms, giving the local school twenty-eight snow days when the average was two.

In addition to making life miserable for my "warm-blooded" family, the cold winter caused us to spend hundreds of thousands of dollars on organic hay to feed our cattle instead of the grass they can typically eat for most of the winter.

On top of all of this, one of my key employees and closest friends came down overnight with a major health issue and was hospitalized. He was out of commission for five months, which put a severe crimp on our operations at Beyond Organic. There were many moments when it looked like the very dream that God gave me seemed to be coming to an end. No matter what I did or what I said, it wasn't enough.

On another dark night, I stepped outside our modest cabin and looked into the sky again. I reminded myself that Joseph had looked upon the same stars at one time. If Joseph could persevere through trials and setbacks, I could too.

As I write *The Joseph Blessing*, the jury is still out regarding my dream to provide physical salvation and healing to the world. I'm fine with where the Lord has my family and me. Change has been challenging yet good for us. We downsized from a 7,800-square-foot home in the center of paradise— South Florida—and moved a thousand miles to a simple 1,300-square-foot ranch cabin that's a good fifteen-minute drive from the nearest town, a hamlet called Koshnokong, Missouri, population 212.

We live in a place where there's no restaurant I can eat at and no health food store within reasonable driving distance. A place where ticks and flies love human skin. A place where subzero temperatures happen in winter. A place where I'm feeding chickens, nursing baby goats, and shoveling manure seven days a week.

From the time Joseph was thrown into the pit until he became Pharaoh's right-hand man, thirteen years passed. I've spent half that time walking out the dreams that God has given me since 2008. Even though there have been times when I haven't felt like praising God or times when I felt that my happiness and joy were sucked out of me, I've always known that God is in control. All I can do is honor Him, speak my dream, and believe one day that despite what circumstances show, the God who delivered me from Crohn's disease and cancer is the same God who can deliver me from my current challenges. He can fulfill the dreams He's given me and use me to change lives just like He did with Joseph.

I'm still believing God put a dream inside of me. I know the enemy wants to snatch it away. Without impossibility, God can't work a miracle, and without a death—an actual gut-wrenching, tear-jerking, and flesh-tearing death—there can't be a resurrection.

I believe if you want to see God work in your life, especially if He's given you a dream, you have to be prepared that things won't work out the way you think they will. If you look at every great man and woman in the Bible, you'll see that when they were asked to do something or be a part of a God-sized dream, their dreams almost always turned into nightmares. The same thing was happening to me. I understand that God may ask me to sacrifice my dream, just like He asked Abraham to sacrifice Isaac. He may ask the same of you.

But I also believe the God who gave you and me our dreams will bring them to fruition. He will cause our

God-given dreams to change the world, as shown by my good friend Dr. Pete Sulack's story in the next chapter.

Just as God turned an Egyptian house slave into the second most powerful man in Pharaoh's court, the Lord is turning a Tennessee chiropractor into an internationally known evangelist.

And it all began with a vision that God gave him in the African country of Tanzania.

4

A VISION TO A BLESSING

They were running!

Everywhere I (Dr. Pete Sulack) looked, I saw people of all ages racing in my direction. I stood on a portable stage erected in the middle of a huge field outside of Kurnool, one of central India's major cities. A crowd estimated at 125,000 had gathered that evening, tripling expectations. As a sea of humanity swarmed in my direction, tears welled up in my eyes. Trailing behind the faster teens were moms clutching children and gray-haired grandparents, jogging as fast as their weary legs would take them. They were coming by the thousands to receive Jesus!

Here in the heated plains of India, where the temperature was a muggy 98 degrees at 9:30 p.m., I experienced a refreshing breeze that felt like the portals of heaven had opened.

After I shared the Gospel message and invited everyone within the sound of my voice to come forward and receive Jesus Christ as their Lord and Savior, I saw locals *sprinting* in my direction. From the middle of the open field to the sides, and from as far as I could see, a massive crowd swelled with emotion in response to the call to change their lives and accept eternal life with Jesus.

They surged like a tidal wave, massing in front of the stage. Meanwhile, a blue-robed choir behind me, two hundred strong, stirred the audience by lifting their voices into the evening sky. Was this the sound of heaven? I thought so.

Only an all-knowing and all-powerful God could orchestrate what I was witnessing. The fact that thousands of dark-skinned Indians were responding to an altar call presented by a tall, lanky white man from Minnesota didn't seem possible. Was I dreaming? If so, anyone was invited to pinch me.

Local pastors on the stage got out of their chairs to have a closer look at the throng rolling in our direction. A few made circling dance steps, they were so excited. Of those who came forward, a handful were invited to come up on the stage while the choir continued to sing uplifting worship songs.

I witnessed miracles before my very eyes. I saw one woman with scaly skin covered in blisters and boils huddle with one of the pastors for prayer. When she opened her eyes, she was surprised to see her skin turn as soft as a baby's bottom. She could barely contain herself as she praised God even more. Another gentlemen screamed in joy as he realized he could see out of his right eye, which had been blind since birth. A small boy, with an incredulous look on his face, touched his ears because he was hearing for the first time. In the pandemonium prompted by the healings, other shouts of joy rang out. The lame could walk, the deaf could hear, and the blind could see.

What I was witnessing that humid evening was a blessing—a Joseph Blessing—that began three years earlier when I was given a vision that I would travel around the world evangelizing others with the message of God's salvation. My vision—a dream, if you will—happened in Arusha, Tanzania, on my first international missions trip. The year was 2004. It all began when my home church was looking for volunteers to assist an evangelistic team during a ten-day swing through Tanzania, an east African country that lies on the Indian Ocean just below the Equator.

I was up for the adventure. My interest in foreign missions stemmed from stories my grandmother, Dorothea, shared with me while growing up in the Twin Cities area of Minneapolis-St. Paul. Grandma was born in Kohima, Nagaland, in India, the daughter of missionary parents who'd settled in this Indian state situated in the far northeastern corner of the second most populous country in the world. Grandma lived in India the first twelve years of life.

Her parents—my great-grandparents, Joseph and Mabel Tanquist—had literally risked their necks because Nagaland was dominated by tribes known for following primordial customs and brutal traditions, the foremost being the practice of headhunting. For thirty-plus years, my great-grandparents shared the gospel and worked among the local people.

During a lifetime of service, my great-grandparents were instrumental in helping change a culture that was heavily invested in shamans and worshiping spirits of various persuasions into a joyous people who gladly received the Good News of Jesus Christ. Today, more than 90 percent of the Naga people claim to follow Christ as their Lord and Savior.

Perhaps that's why foreign missions was in my DNA. When my home church was looking for volunteers to go to Tanzania for an evangelistic mission trip, I was up for the adventure. My wife, Stephanie, encouraged me to go, even though that meant she'd have to stay behind with our two boys and a third on the way.

One evening in Tanzania, I attended an outdoor crusade in Arusha, a city of more than one million in the northern part of the African country. The 25,000 people who showed up that night were the biggest crowd I'd ever seen at an evangelistic event. Arusha was a multicultural city in a country where Islam and animism—the belief that all creatures and all objects have a soul or personality—were the predominant religions.

That night in a large field, I saw hundreds, if not thousands, come forward to give their lives to Christ. I was deeply impacted to witness this movement of God, as was everyone in my church group who came over for the trip. When the evening's crusade was finished, we returned to our hotel, still on a high about what happened.

Around ten of us gathered in one of our hotel rooms to wind down. We were on the third floor, chatting away, having fun, when someone said, "What would happen if we really sought the Lord diligently for the next ten minutes and laid hands on one person?"

The hotel room got quiet. An instant later, I heard myself say, "Give it to me."

One of our church leaders directed me over to a king-sized bed in the hotel room. I sat on one end of the bed as the others gathered around. I felt hands come upon my head and shoulders, and the next thing I knew, I was lying on my back, looking at the ceiling. I closed my eyes and prayed, *Lord, if there is something You want for me, I want that. I don't want to leave anything on the table. Give it to me.*

That's the way I'd always been. My attitude was that I didn't want to get to heaven someday knowing that I had missed something the Lord wanted me to do here on earth. In other words, I didn't want to settle as a millionaire in God's economy when I could have been a billionaire.

While lying on my back, I had an encounter with the Lord. There's no other way to describe it.

During that time, He told me that certain people in Nagaland, India had been praying for me for years, asking the Lord to order my steps according to His will.

I was floored to hear that people who didn't know me, halfway across the globe, had lifted up prayers of intercession on my behalf. Then I heard the Lord say, *This is what I'm going to do in your life.*

In this dream, I was barefoot, walking on the greenest grass I'd ever seen, but it wasn't grass. It was more like a moss—a soft moss that scrunches up through your toes. I looked to the side and saw Jesus. He was wearing a robe that wasn't white but more pearlescent. He extended His hand, and I put my hand into His. Suddenly, I saw a window open up to my left. Through the window, I could see the planet Earth, as if we were in outer space.

"Lord, what are You showing me?" I asked.

"I'm giving you the nations of the earth."

We began to walk a little further, hand in hand. Once again, a new window opened up. This time, I saw tens of thousands of people surrounding a stage in a large field, much like I had witnessed that night in Arusha. Everywhere I looked, I saw people as far as the eye can see.

"Jesus, is this the crusade we're at?"

"No, it's not."

"But that's You on the stage," I said. Standing on the platform was the Lord Jesus, dressed exactly as He looked now.

"No, son, that's *you*, but they see Me."

I was blown away. Before I knew it, we were in the middle of the huge crowd. We walked through a glorious white fog accentuated by brightly colored crystals swirling in the air, much like the confetti that's unfurled when a world champion is crowned at the Super Bowl or NCAA championship football game.

The white fog was like the glory of God, and I had a sense of His presence that was magnified by the red, orange, and yellow crystals that speckled in the midst of this white cloud. Then I saw individuals come out of the thick, white mass and approach me.

"What's happening?" I asked the first, a woman in her forties.

"I was blind and now I see."

Next I saw someone my age. "I was lost, but now I'm found," he said.

Each person who moved toward me uttered the same thing—he or she had been set free by Christ and was healed and delivered.

"Lord, this is amazing," I said.

Then I took a second look at the stage—and now saw myself.

"Lord, why do I see myself now?"

"I have called you to see one hundred million souls come to Me though live events that you'll conduct and a billion souls through the media."

With that, my dream came to an end.

I was later told that I had lain on my back on the hotel bed for four hours. My friends were transfixed by what I went through. No one moved in the hotel room, but they continued to pray for me. I didn't know that four hours passed in a blur.

Like the apostle Paul said in 2 Corinthians 12:2, whether I was in my body or out of my body, I did not know. Only one thing I knew for sure: I had been with Jesus.

Every once in a while, I would wake up with a Scripture that the Lord gave me. I believe He brought me into this realm that was above the earth, and it was angelic and evil at the same time. It was the greatest feeling and the worst feeling.

"Lord, what is this place?"

"This is the spirit realm where angels and demons reside. When you speak the Word of God, the angels are released to bring forth My Word. Why? To bring glory to My Father in heaven. But when you speak contrary to the Word of God, it gives access to the demonic realm. Speak the Word of God, or don't speak at all."

I was twenty-eight years old at the time of my dream. I'd never had a supernatural encounter with the Lord like that—and haven't since. The beauty, the details, and the textures were nothing like this world offers. Sights and words in our vocabulary are inadequate to describe what I saw in my semi-conscious state.

I heard the Lord say one more thing to me: "When you turn twenty-nine, it will be a year of intimacy and preparation. And when you turn thirty, I'll release you to the nations."

I wasn't sure exactly what the Lord meant, but I knew He was serious. When I turned twenty-nine on January 12, 2005,

I felt Him telling me to fast every Monday, Wednesday, and Friday that year. Not out of any sense of legalism or a belief that fasting three days a week would set me on a pedestal. I had fasted before, and I'll be quite frank with you: it was brutal. But the Lord was clearly giving me a directive.

I want you to become intimate with Me. I want you to begin hearing My voice more clearly, He said.

For an entire year, I fasted every Monday, Wednesday, and Friday. For good measure, I did a twenty-one day fast three times. Sometimes I drank only water, sometimes I added juice. I didn't eat during the day and into the evening, although some nights I had dinner with my family.

I had amazing results. I'm a chiropractor, so I'd pray for my patients. On the days I fasted, I'd hear my patients say things like, "How did you know that was happening in my life?"

There were occasions where we did devotions at the office before we started seeing patients. I led most of the mini Bible studies, which meant I stood up before my employees and spoke about a certain Scripture and what God was trying to teach us. I'll admit that I really got into it. You could say I was preaching.

At any rate, I had a patient come into the office. He'd been a missionary posted all over the world, and he knew about my heritage in India. He thought I'd be interested in supporting a children's home in India that was trying to raise money to buy a cow to feed the orphaned kids. "Could you give us twenty-five dollars?" he asked.

That seemed like a modest amount for a worthy cause. "Sure," I replied. "Let me get you a check."

I excused myself and walked along the hallway to my office. Before I opened the door, I heard the Lord speak to me: *Give him a blank check.*

"What, Lord?"

Give him a blank check. Let him fill out the amount.

I shrugged my shoulders. It was the Lord speaking. I felt compelled to obey.

When I returned, I said, "Here, take this," handing my missionary friend a blank draft with my signature. "Just let me know what the final amount is to get the kids their needed cow." (The amount turned out to be somewhere around $500.)

Not long after that, I received a phone call from my missionary friend. "Hey, Dr. Pete. I was speaking with Bishop Ernest, and he'd like you to come to India," he said.

"Who's Bishop Ernest?"

I found out that he was a very influential man in world missions. Dr. Ernest Paul Komanapalli was founder and head of Manna International, which operated more than three dozen children's homes in India with 3,500 children under their care. Manna International also operated four Bible schools, fifteen elementary and high schools, two vocational schools, a college, three clinics, and a thirty-bed hospital.

Bishop Ernest was also chairman of Pentecostal World Fellowship and was the go-to man when evangelists like

Franklin Graham, Reinhard Bonnke, and T.L. Osborne needed boots on the ground when embarking on a crusade on foreign shores.

When I spoke with Bishop Ernest on the phone, he invited me to come to India to get the lay of the land. Half a year later, I was sitting in his office in Hyderabad, India, getting to know this bespectacled man in his sixties with salt-and-pepper hair. We met only three weeks after a massive undersea earthquake with a magnitude of 9.1 unleashed a devastating tsunami in the Indian Ocean on December 26, 2004. An estimated 250,000 people died when a wall of water swept into low-lying areas in Thailand, Indonesia, Sri Lanka, and India's Tamil Nadu region.

We were having a friendly chat when the phone rang.

I listened to Bishop Ernest speak in Telagu. Suddenly, a look of grave concern covered his expansive face. When he was finished, he set the phone down.

"That was a colleague of mine from the Tamil Nadu area. They found 105 children wandering the beach, looking for their missing parents. It's the saddest thing, what this tsunami has done."

My heart suddenly starting beating through my chest. The Lord's voice was undeniable: Offer to take care of the financial responsibilities of the children and the children's home.

I had no idea what that would cost, but I heard myself saying, "Bishop Ernest, could I take care of that children's home?" I didn't know what it was going to cost me, but that didn't matter. It was God's money. I would ask others to help financially.

That became our first children's home, and the reason I say "our" is because upon my return to the U.S., I started a nonprofit ministry called Matthew 10 International, which we dedicated to proclaiming the Good News of Jesus Christ, serving widows and orphans, ministering to the sick, and empowering pastors and leaders.

There's one more thing I want to mention about my visit with Bishop Ernest. During our time together, the Lord spoke to him, saying, *This is the man to talk to India about Jesus Christ. He is the vessel for India.*

Before I left for the airport for my return trip to the States, Bishop Ernest pulled me aside. "I want you to come back and speak at an evangelistic crusade that we're planning for later this summer."

"But...but I've never preached in public before," I said. "I'm just a chiropractor from Tennessee."

Bishop Ernest waved off my concerns. "The Lord has given you an anointing. Don't worry. Just speak from your heart. He will tell you what to say."

Six months later, I was standing on a portable stage in Rajahmundry, one of the major cities in the state of Andhra Pradesh. Before me, a sea of dark-skinned faces waited with expectation for me to present the Gospel. This was the third and last night of the crusade.

I had notes prepared, but I discarded them after the Lord told me, *Don't preach healing. Preach the simple gospel.*

That's what I did.

When thousands started running to the stage, I felt like it was the start of the fulfillment of the dream I had in Tanzania—the one in which the Lord said I would see 100 million souls accept Christ into their hearts and a billion souls through the media. Just as the Lord had promised, the Indians had responded to my clear presentation of their need for Christ. The crusade was a resounding success.

Afterward, Bishop Ernest told me, "You know what? I took a huge risk bringing you here. You are a nobody. But the Lord spoke to me and said, 'He is the man for India.'"

Bishop Ernest was right. I was a nobody.

But the Lord had given me a dream that had been building all my life.

Like Joseph, I'm not afraid to share that dream.

MY EARLY YEARS

My mom will tell you firsthand that I was a quiet, shy, and introverted child growing up in Shoreview, Minnesota, a suburb of the Twin Cities of Minneapolis-St. Paul. Some say I have a Lake Wobegon accent, a reflection of my Swedish and Norwegian heritage. One of my earliest childhood memories was always being served a mild Indian curry dish when Grandma came over for holiday gatherings.

When I was a young kid, my dad was a basketball coach at Northwestern Bible College, where Billy Graham was hired as president in 1947 at the age of thirty, making him the youngest person to serve as president of any U.S. college or university at the time. Dr. Graham's preaching ministry exploded after the Los Angeles crusades in 1949, and shortly thereafter, he left Northwestern to pursue where God was leading him, and that was evangelizing souls around the world.

I was in sixth grade when my dad also left Northwestern, not to preach the gospel but to train church planters. Even though he was no longer coaching basketball at the collegiate level, he instilled a love for the game within my younger brother, Mike, and me. We had a basketball hoop in the driveway, so there were spirited two-on-two and three-on-three games with other kids in the neighborhood.

I really thought I was destined to play in the NBA, but doesn't every kid who's crazy about basketball? If I didn't play, then I'd coach basketball like Dad or my grandfather Chuck, who passed away before I was born but put together a very successful high school coaching career, winning eight Minnesota state titles.

I played for Mounds View High in Shoreview, but injuries limited my playing time. I was always getting roughed up under the boards because I was tall and lanky, rising to six feet five inches, but weighing only 185 pounds. Even though I didn't have a lot of bulk, I held my own on the court. I wasn't good enough to play Division 1 ball, but Bethel University, a small Christian college a few miles away in St. Paul, wanted me to play for them.

The best part about playing at Bethel was that my parents could watch all my home games. I started as a freshman and sophomore, but I was insecure on the court, an outgrowth of my shy personality. I wasn't the type of player who had to be The Guy—the Michael Jordan ultra-competitor who took over the fourth quarter. I was your hustling gym rat who played hard-nosed defense and hit the open jumper. A team player.

Back problems and headaches plagued my junior and senior years, and I barely played at all. That was really frustrating, but God used that time in ways that greatly impacted what I do today and the family I have. For instance, my back problems on the basketball court led me to pursue a doctoral degree in chiropractic. (Reality also set in because I had learned that coaching basketball wasn't going to pay the bills.) Choosing to become a pre-med student kept me in the school library, where I met my future wife.

During my sophomore year, I was studying in the school library when I looked up and saw a beautiful young woman with shiny blonde hair sitting at a computer. She took my breath away. She was the finest-looking woman I'd ever seen in my life.

She was doing research on some type of project. For two hours, I stole glances and worked up the courage to approach her and say something. Out of the corner of her eye, I think she noticed me, but she didn't let on.

Finally, I mustered up the courage to introduce myself. With my heart booming in my chest, I walked up to her and gave her one of the greatest pick-up lines ever. "So, what are you doing? Working on the computer?"

I know. Pretty lame. She looked at me like I was an idiot. "Yeah, I'm working on a computer, and you've been watching me for the last two hours."

And then she smiled, letting me know she was okay with the goofy guy who'd been checking her out.

Stephanie Vreeman and I dated for six months and then got engaged. We were married a year later on June 27, 1997, at the end of my junior year. After graduation, I enrolled at Northwestern College of Chiropractic in Bloomington, Minnesota, about a half hour southwest of where I grew up.

After I became a doctor of chiropractic, we moved to Knoxville, Tennessee, where I went into practice. The first of four boys, Isaiah, was born in January 1999. Life got incredibly busy as my practice exploded. I was seeing patients one after another. They'd line up in the hallway for their adjustments. By the world's standards, I experienced great success, but Stephanie and I agreed that the Lord was blessing us with financial resources that should be used to further His kingdom. That's why she readily agreed when I proposed being a part of our church's mission trip to Tanzania in 2004.

Since my experience in Arusha and the launch of Matthew 10 International Ministries, I've done fifteen crusades in places like India, Argentina, Venezuela, and Nigeria, presenting Jesus. I've spoken in Cartagena, Columbia, one of the most vicious drug-cartel cities in the world, but also one of the ripest fields. People back home ask me if I'm afraid to go places where many are hostile to the Gospel. I say if God is for me, there is nothing that can stand against me. When it's a dream from the Lord, I'm His.

What my dream did was place a *knowing* passion within me for the nations of the earth. My dream has set the course of my life ever since that night in Arusha. I didn't choose this, but like the apostle Paul said, "He chose us."

You, too, have been chosen just like Jordan and myself, but being called by God isn't always smooth sailing. In fact, during the next few chapters, you will realize that it's quite the contrary. In my situation, my dream didn't change my profession. I'm still a chiropractor today, but I've had to—wanted to—make adjustments in my professional as well as personal life to preach the Gospel around the world.

Together, Jordan and I want to encourage you to discover the Joseph Blessing in your life. For Joseph, it happened while he slept. For me, it happened in a Tanzanian hotel room. For Jordan, it happened while he rode the Perfect Weight America tour bus across amber waves of GMO grain. For the both of us, we're 100 percent sure that the Lord has given Jordan a dream to provide starving people with physical food/salvation and myself a dream to provide starving souls with spiritual food/salvation.

Your Joseph dream could happen when you're at work or at home. It might happen at the altar. Or maybe your dream is something God gave you as a young child, and you have been carrying it around ever since. Whatever way the Joseph Blessing begins in your life—or might start for you some day in the future—the way your dream occurs is not significant.

What is significant and imperative to know is this: the Joseph dream will happen if you ask God to use you to change the world.

MOVING AHEAD

It's our belief that we are living in a unique time in history when we need an army of Josephs to be raised up to deliver God's people from the "Egypt" of this modern world—a popular culture that dismisses God as irrelevant, celebrates apostasy, indulges in every kind of sin, threatens to destroy the fiber of our faith, steals the integrity of our health, and rob us of our financial freedom. When you walk in the Joseph Blessing, however, you'll discover:

- your identity
- your purpose
- your legacy

You can change the world with your God-given dream and influence those around you in ways you never thought possible. Whether you're a homeschooling mom, an employee in a factory, a CEO of a Fortune 500 company, a pastor, or a doctor, if you call on the name of the Lord, He will give you His dream for your life. He will orchestrate your steps if you dare to live out your dream and honor Him.

When that happens, you'll be following in the path set by a young man who wasn't afraid to share his dreams. Not once did Joseph step back from his firm belief that the God of his fathers—Abraham, Isaac, and Jacob—had a plan for his life.

Even though Joseph was sold into slavery, imprisoned on a trumped-up charge, and forgotten by the cup bearer who said he'd try to get him released, he bounced back and was responsible for saving the nation of Israel during a time of severe famine. Joseph was also the catalyst for populating the Hebrew people in Egypt, which led to oppression by Pharaoh but also the amazing story of the Exodus and the trek to the Promised Land—thereby setting the stage for the arrival of the Messiah, born in Bethlehem centuries later.

Joseph believed God sent him to preserve a posterity by saving his family from famine through a "great deliverance" (Genesis 45:7). As he told his brothers, "So now it was not you who sent me here [to Egypt], but God; and He has made me a father to Pharaoh, and lord of all his house, and a ruler throughout all the land of Egypt" (Genesis 45:8).

Joseph was a blessing to others, and that's a direct result of his dream. You, too, can be a blessing to others. To help you get there, we've prepared seven steps you can take to change the world with your God-given dream. They are:

1. Believe that you are His favorite.

2. Embrace your God-given dream.

3. Navigate through the nightmare.

4. Don't birth Ishmael.

5. Lay down your Isaac.

6. Walk in His Spirit.

7. Allow God to be God.

In the following chapters, Jordan and I will expand on these seven steps that will help prepare you to walk in the Joseph Blessing.

Before you turn the page, keep this thought first and foremost inside your heart: When you seek Him, dwell in the secret place, and abide with Him, He will give you the desires of your heart. He's just waiting to give you the same blessing He bestowed upon Joseph.

All you have to do is dream.

5

BELIEVE THAT YOU ARE HIS FAVORITE

Now Israel [Jacob] *loved Joseph more than all his children, because he was the son of his old age* (Genesis 37:3).

THE STORY OF JOSEPH IS ONE OF THE GREATEST DEPICTIONS of God's divine plan for someone's life, from the inception of a vision to the fulfillment and manifestation of that ideal. We see similar plans laid out in the lives of Abraham, David, and others throughout Scripture, which highlights how the living God desires to work in each of our lives. The Joseph Blessing can be a roadmap to your destiny.

In the next seven chapters, we're going to unpack the seven steps to walk in the Joseph Blessing that we laid out in the previous chapter. As you seek to be used by God to change the world with your God-given dream, keep these ideas in mind:

- God uses your identity, or who you are, as He shapes your dream.

- Following your dream to change the world around you often leads to persecution.

- Persecution confirms you are following God.

- Facing the death of your dream is a reminder that we cannot do anything in our own strength. This means...

- To have the greatest strength, you must surrender to Him, and...

- Once you surrender to Him, you will find fulfillment and purpose while experiencing the Joseph Blessing, wherever it takes you in life.

Let's discuss the first step to changing the world, which is this: *Believe you are His favorite.*

The concept of believing that you are God's favorite is difficult for many people, and rightly so. You may have grown up in a home where you were belittled, put down, and ignored. You were *nobody's* favorite and not the apple of your parents' eye.

Or perhaps you've been beaten down by life, or maybe you've messed things up so many times that you've lost count. Under scenarios like these, it would be difficult to see yourself in a positive light. You have trouble believing that you're special to *anyone*, let alone God.

We want you to realize that you were made from His workmanship, created in Christ Jesus for good works (Ephesians 2:10). You should feel great confidence walking in Him because He knows how many hair follicles are on your head and says you are more valuable than many sparrows (Luke 12:7). The idea of having a unique relationship with Jesus should fill your sails because your relationship *is* personal and up close.

But let's say that you grew up in a good home with loving, attentive parents and a couple of brothers and sisters. Your father and mother were probably told in parenting class to be careful about not showing favoritism among the children, so they assiduously made sure they treated you and your siblings "fairly." They were careful not to express any preference for one child over another in keeping with the spirit of impartiality.

Believe it or not, that's not how our heavenly Father treats us. In ways we cannot understand because we are human and He is not, each of us is His favorite child. That means you are His favorite, which I'm glad to see. But I am His favorite, too. Your spouse or close family member is His favorite. When you consider that there are more than 7 billion people on this planet who are uniquely special to God, that's an awesome truth to contemplate.

But we want you to *focus* on the revelation that you are His favorite. If you clutch this truth, you will want to spend time with Him, which will bring you closer to the Lord and deepen your relationship with Him. Who wouldn't want to spend time with Someone—in worship and in prayer—who considers you to be His favorite?

I (Dr. Pete) have had a teeny glimpse into what it's like for Jesus to love each and every one of us in this way. When Stephanie gave birth to our first child, Isaiah, I was twenty-three years old. It's safe to say that I had no clue on how to be a father or what parenting would be like.

After a long labor, things progressed quickly inside the birthing room. Suddenly, the obstetrician announced, "It's a boy," and I was holding a wiggly infant boy in my arms. The reality could not be more stark: I was his father, and he was my son. The torch had been passed from one generation to the next.

I can remember feeling a surge of supernatural love come out of me. I had no idea where my cherishing love for Isaiah came from, but it had to be from the Lord Himself. I began to love this kid more than anything I could ever imagine in my whole life. He was mine, and I was his.

A couple of years later, Stephanie was in the latter stages of her second pregnancy. I remember her saying, "How can I love anyone as much as I love Isaiah?" I felt the same way, but when Eli arrived with a full-throated cry, I instantly loved him as much as I loved Isaiah. The same thing happened with the births of Ashton and Ezekiel. The love within me doubled, tripled, and quadrupled. Stephanie felt the same way.

As much as my heart bursts with love for my four sons, it doesn't compare to Jesus' love for me. It can't. Christ's love knows no boundaries. Jesus made it clear that He died for you and for me, and He would have allowed Himself to be crucified if just one of us had sinned just one time. Therefore, we are His favorite.

Admittedly, this is a hard concept to grasp, but it's true. God says that He didn't die for the world but that He died for each and every one of us.

Which makes each of us His favorite.

FROM JORDAN'S SIDE

I (Jordan) have a bit of a different perspective than Dr. Pete because I'm an adoptive father. You've heard it said that adoptive parents feel the same incredible love for their adopted children, but for Nicki and me, we had to hold our emotions in check for months because there were complications completing the adoption of our son Samuel. Once the legal process was cleared up—which took a good six months—our hearts opened even wider. That's normal in an adoptive situation.

From a godly perspective, we are not adopted by Christ. We are His, and we are His favorite. I know my Lord and Savior's heart is wide open for me. I rest in the knowledge that I am His and He is mine. I have an advocate who fights with me and for me. I've seen Him do that time and again in my adult life, especially after He was incredibly close to me during my fight to stay alive in my early twenties. He has said that the battle is not ours but His, and I believe that He has fought for me in ways I never thought possible, and that's because I am His favorite.

If you don't believe that you are God's favorite, it'll be easy to become discouraged when things aren't bouncing your way. But you're the apple of His eye, chosen by Him. His favoritism for you isn't a fluke.

Dr. Pete and I were both fortunate to grow up in homes with a father. We understand that's not a given these days. You may have a skewed idea about a father figure, or feel uneasy being a dad in a popular culture where fatherhood is put down every night in TV sitcoms.

Jesus, as your Father, wants you to believe that you are His favorite. Take that step of faith, even if your earthly father was AWOL or not the father he should have been. If you don't know you're the favorite of God, there won't be any attraction for you to seek His face. Let Him be the foundation of everything you're going to do. Let Him sustain you through the journey. Let Him walk you through the fire that comes. Know that you are His favorite.

It may take some practice to get there. Eventually, we want you to reach a point where you are "unconsciously competent" in who you are and whose you are.

What do we mean by becoming unconsciously competent?

It's a phrase that relates to four levels of learning. The first level is being *unconsciously incompetent*. That's means you don't know that you don't know.

Let's use an example from everyday life. When you were two years old and starting to run around like crazy, you didn't even know that you should know how to tie your shoes. You were "unconsciously incompetent" in the task, as all toddlers are.

Then you grew a little older and realized that sneakers fit better when the shoelaces were tied up and done. You were a preschooler who was *consciously incompetent* and aware that you didn't know how to tie your shoes. So that's why you asked Mom to tie your little Nikes.

Then you hit kindergarten, a time when every kid learns to tie his shoes, some better than others. So you learn how to take the right lace and cross it over the left lace and then form a loop and hold it with your right index finger and thumb close to the shoe. There are more steps until you can pull on both loops until they are tight, which leads us to the third level, which is *consciously competent*. That means you can tie your shoes, but you're inexperienced enough at the task that you still have to think about how you do it.

Kids are quick learners, so it usually doesn't take them long to reach the fourth level, which is *unconsciously competent*. This means you can tie your shoes without thinking how to do it. It's rote. You can tie your shoes anytime and anywhere without getting flustered about whether you'll remember the right way to do it.

In a similar fashion with the Joseph Blessing, we want you to become "unconsciously competent" in your walk with Christ. When you've reached the point where you're super comfortable that you are His and He is yours, then you don't even think about where you stand with the Lord. You know that you are His favorite.

Which leads us to our final point: Your identity in Christ breeds activity, and when you're active as a Christian, you're doing activities that bear fruit.

Knowing that you are God's favorite should take a boatload of pressure off your shoulders.

THE JOSEPH BLESSING PRAYER

At the end of each of the seven steps, we would like you to repeat a prayer that we have written for you. Actually, we'd like you to say this prayer several times each day until completing the next chapter of this book so that the words can marinate in your heart. The power of our words is important, so join us in confessing this prayer:

Lord, thank You that I'm Your favorite. Open up the eyes of my understanding that I may know You more and more each day. Show me how deep and wide Your love is for me.

6

EMBRACE YOUR DREAM

Now Joseph had a dream, and he told it to his brothers;
and they hated him even more (Genesis 37:5).

ONE THING WE'VE LEARNED IS THAT THROUGHOUT HISTORY,
God has given His children dreams and visions of how He
would change the world through them as they surrendered
themselves to Him. Even our Lord and Savior Jesus Christ
shared a vision of the future with Peter, James, and his brother
John when He led them up a high mountain and was trans-
figured before them. "His face shone like the sun, and His
clothes became as white as the light," Scripture tells us. "Now
as they came down from the mountain, Jesus commanded
them, saying, 'Tell the vision to no one until the Son of Man
is risen from the dead'" (Matthew 17:2b, 9).

It all started with a dream for Joseph. Have you ever had a fantastic dream—a dream so vivid and real that you could almost taste it, touch it, and feel it? A dream so wild that you couldn't tell anybody because you feared you'd be laughed at? Or people would think you're crazy?

I (Jordan) love the following story because it illustrates how my oldest son, Joshua, embraced his dream and wouldn't let up until Nicki and I said yes.

It all began a couple of years ago when Joshua was eight years old. The Lord gave him *eight* dreams over an eleven-day period. Call it a spiritual awakening of sorts.

One evening, when Nicki was putting Joshua to bed, he told her that he had a dream the previous night.

"What kind of dream?" she asked.

"Last night, God spoke to me in my brain and told me that it's time to start the children's home today."

I learned about this dream when I returned home from a business trip. His description blew us away considering Joshua had never told us about any vivid dreams before, much less a dream in which God spoke to him. Nicki and I had talked before about the idea that the Lord was leading us to help children in need, so Joshua knew this could be a future possibility.

Then a few days later, while driving in the car, Joshua informed us that the Lord had spoken to him in another dream. "We're going to India," he announced in a matter-of-fact way.

This conversation happened in the spring of 2012 after Dr. Pete came by our house to tell us about his next evangelistic trip. It's possible that Joshua may have over-heard some "adult talk" about the upcoming crusade to India, but we hadn't breathed a word to Joshua or his siblings that we were seriously considering joining Dr. Pete in India. The trip was eight months away, and we hadn't purchased airline tickets yet.

Just to make sure she heard right, Nicki asked, "Who's we?"

"Me, you, and Dad," Joshua responded.

"But you don't have a passport."

"Then let's get me one."

Out of the mouth of babes.

Nicki and I hadn't thought of bringing our third-grade son to a Third World country like India. Let's face it, this wasn't a "kid's trip," and no one his age had *ever* been a part of one of Dr. Pete's crusades. At the same time, we couldn't discount the fact that God had told him in a dream that he was going to India with us.

When I spoke with Joshua, I could tell that he embraced the idea of traveling a long, long distance to witness Dr. Pete presenting Jesus Christ at a large outdoor field with tens of thousands of people. He didn't want to go as a tourist to see how people lived in India and try some spicy food. He wanted to see Dr. Pete win souls for Christ.

We checked with Dr. Pete, who gave us a thumb's up for the trip in early December 2012. Even though the journey from South Florida to southeastern India was as grueling as we expected, more than twenty-seven hours from our front door to the home we stayed in, our son more than held his own in the twelve-person contingent from America.

But as I mentioned earlier, this was just one of his eight dreams. Our son is intelligent, and he knew that a children's home was a place for young kids who were orphaned or abandoned by their parents. His dream that we would open a children's home is greatly influencing our lives today, even though his dream has yet to be fully realized.

When he told us about this dream in 2012, we already owned the large parcels of property in southern Missouri, but we never planned to permanently move to the ranch. We had a team of employees—modern day cowboys, if you will— taking care of the herds and working the land. When friends asked us if we ever thought of moving to Missouri, my stock answer was this: "We have no immediate plans to live there. We'd only move if things got really bad."

Nicki's reaction was stronger: "God has to speak to me before I'll move." She said she doesn't like bugs, she doesn't like dirt, and she doesn't like thousand-square-foot cabins. Nicki likes nice things. Who can blame her? She loved where we lived and loved how nice, clean health food stores were close by. It's pretty comfy living in Palm Beach Gardens.

But when Joshua said he had a dream in which God told him that we needed to open a children's home, *that* changed our thinking. Perhaps Missouri *was* where God was leading us. After all, He had given me a dream to purchase lands where I could own cattle, raise my own food, and provide shelter for my family and others in times of need. Maybe we were supposed to add a children's home to the mix.

Two weeks after Joshua's dream, the Lord spoke clearly to me during a praise and worship time that we would be leaving our beloved home and moving to Missouri—the first step toward opening a children's home. Following much prayer, wise counsel, and seeking the Lord, both Nicki and I felt the nudge in our backs to pick up stakes in South Florida and move the family a thousand miles to Missouri. We embraced these dreams because we knew they were coming from God. What He was leading us to do was something we'd never choose for ourselves or ever accomplish on our own. Nicki will definitely tell you that God revealed Himself to her in visions and dreams regarding the move to Missouri.

Meanwhile, Joshua is adamant that we will have a children's home someday, but we're taking baby steps to get there. Until then, I believe God is working on this big time behind the scenes. Even as I write this, we could be receiving our second new child!

What I like regarding Joshua's dream is that he didn't have a dream about what he was going to be when he grew up or some exciting toy he wanted. Instead, he had a dream about opening a children's home that cannot be accomplished on his own strength. It is a God-sized dream.

The theme here is that Joshua had a dream that he was willing to talk about and proclaim to anyone who would listen. As for the dream God has given me—to be a Joseph—I think all God wants is for me to be willing. I believe I've done that, despite how bleak things have looked at times. Regardless of how truly impossible this dream looks, I continue to proclaim it to this day and won't stop until it comes to pass.

DREAMS CAN BE DIVINE

Another way to define the word *dreams* is to call them "divine revelations."

We don't want to imply that every dream you have comes straight from the Lord as some sort of godly disclosure. But when you seek Him, abide in Him, and dwell in His secret place, He will give you the desires of your heart, which may come through a dream that He plants in your consciousness.

The Father easily has the ability to place an assignment or destiny in your spirit through a dream or vision. When you feel like the Lord gives a dream to you, you want to take ownership of that dream because God brought the revelation directly to you. He places the seed within you and makes your vision personal. You're the one responsible for nurturing the dream until He is ready to give birth to something you're passionate about.

This is why others will never be as impassioned about your dream as you will be. It's like when you become a parent with the birth of your first child: no one will love and care for your son or daughter as much as you will, nor would you expect anyone to feel the same way as you. It's the same with the vision that the Lord plants in your heart.

We want you to embrace your dream. If you haven't received a direct revelation from God, that's fine. Be patient and embrace the waiting, but be on the lookout for the dream God has destined for you.

If you're thinking that you're too old to have a dream or God's never given you a dream before so why should He start now, then recall your childhood. When you were growing up, sometime in your elementary school years, you probably had a dream of what you wanted to become.

I want to become a fireman!

I want to become a doctor!

I want to become a policeman!

I want to become a teacher!

It's interesting how younger children always want to become something when they grow up. Let them believe they can change the world, save lives, or become superheroes. Let their imaginations roam because sometimes childhood dreams spark a lifelong passion. It's marvelous if young boys want to become the next Spiderman or baseball stars like Los Angeles Angels' slugger Mike Trout. It's fine if preschool girls view themselves as queens or princesses and if leotard-clad seven-year-old girls are sure they'll be performing on the uneven bars at the Summer Olympic Games someday.

We're parents of young boys who've put on baseball uniforms and carried their bats and mitts around, pretending their next Little League game is the climactic seventh game of the World Series. Every kid has a dream, whether it's playing ball, zipping through the air on the uneven bars, becoming a firefighter, or getting elected as the next president of the

United States. Maybe you haven't had a dream since you were a kid, but it's never too late. Open your heart to the vision that God can give you. Ask Him for a big, glorious dream that will impact others for the Kingdom.

We believe God has a dream for everyone. You can suppress it. You can avoid it. You can fail trying to see your dream succeed. But it's still yours.

Joseph didn't ask to have his dream that his father and brothers would one day bow to him. He didn't *try* to make his dream happen. He merely went to bed one night, and God laid down such a vivid dream that Joseph was *sure* that God was speaking to him. Receiving a second version of the first dream sealed the deal for him.

No one doubted that Joseph's vision of his family bowing down to him was a powerful, searing image. But it was still unbelievable anyway. Even his father, who favored him the most, said, "Surely you don't mean we're going to bow down to you."

Well, Dad, that's what the dream means.

Joseph embraced his dream, come what may, because he believed that it came from God. If you've been given a dream, then we urge you to embrace it as well. While dreams that God gives us often can't come to fruition unless something supernatural happens, don't discount "little" dreams. For example, if you're a young parent, your dream may be raising children who honor God and won't go astray. That's a wonderful dream! Imagine what the world would look like if every parent pointed their kids in the right direction and followed through with the necessary discipline to teach them the way they should go so that when they are older, they will not depart from it (Proverbs 22:6).

Another Proverb says this: "Where there is no revelation, the people cast off restraint" (Proverbs 29:18), but perhaps the New American Standard Bible says it better for our modern ears: "Where there is no vision, the people are unrestrained."

Without divine revelation, people are like sheep without a shepherd—going any which way. This verse suddenly meant a lot more to me (Jordan) when we moved to the Missouri ranch. We have a large fenced-in area for a small herd of sheep and goats that would be lost without a caretaker and even more lost without someone who has a vision to lead them.

THE DAY OF THE LORD

Each and every night, God is giving people physical dreams. He's giving people visions. We believe there's an upswing in this type of spiritual activity, undergirded by this Scripture:

> *And it shall come to pass afterward that I will pour out My Spirit on all flesh; your sons and your daughters shall prophesy, your old men shall dream dreams, your young men shall see visions* (Joel 2:28).

Writing this book, *The Joseph Blessing,* has been a step of faith that God is supernaturally making something happen among His people.

So you may be asking yourself: How do I know what I experienced is a God-given dream?

Answer: When your dream can result in changed lives and your dream is impossible to accomplish on your own strength.

But sometimes God-given dreams can temporarily turn to nightmares, as we'll explore in our next chapter.

THE JOSEPH BLESSING PRAYER

Lord, You said those who hunger and thirst for You shall be filled. As I seek and delight myself in You today, bring greater revelation to the destiny for my life and let it burn within me.

7

NAVIGATE THE NIGHTMARE

So it came to pass, when Joseph had come to his brothers, that they stripped Joseph of his tunic, the tunic of many colors that was on him. Then they took him and cast him into a pit. And the pit was empty; there was no water in it (Genesis 37:23-24).

EVERYBODY HAS A DREAM—OR AT LEAST DAYDREAMS ABOUT the future.

For the latter, it might be an impending engagement or upcoming wedding. It could be the birth of a child, a promotion at work, or a new career path. Or it could be a fantastic dream that God has given you, which was Joseph's situation.

Joseph had a dream that his brothers would prostrate themselves before him. He spoke his dream. And where did his forthrightness land him? In a deep pit. The very brothers who were supposed to be the closest to him—and have his back—perpetrated this cowardly and despicable act. They had to know that handing him over to Ishmaelite traders put him on a path where life was guaranteed to be tough and short.

Joseph's dream directly led to his nightmare because if he had kept his mouth shut and not told his brothers about his dream, he wouldn't have experienced the nightmare of being left for dead in a pit or dragged off to an uncertain fate in a foreign land.

I (Jordan) was reminded of this during a recent foray on the farm. Dr. Pete and his nine-year-old son, Ashton, drove from Knoxville to Koshnokong to work on *The Joseph Blessing*. The first morning, we drove around on our UTVs—utility terrain vehicles—to look at our cowherd, the prize of years of selective breeding.

My dream is to provide milk and meat to people, and you could say that every hope and dream of this property—at least on the protein side—is wrapped up in our herd. But we noticed something that morning. We were driving through one of the fenced-off paddocks when we saw a cow lying upside down in a hole. Lying next to her was a half-eaten baby calf with its entrails and much of its rear skeleton missing.

Now I know some of you reading this might not like the picture I painted, but what happened illustrates a point I'm about to make. A heifer, or female cow, that gives birth for the first time is called a first-calf heifer. This is a head of cattle that eats, sleeps, and breeds to create and feed herself and the baby calf inside of her. Her only function in life is to reproduce. All her hopes and dreams are bound up in her offspring. For this heifer, the day came and the baby calf was born.

When this mother heifer lay down in the grass to give birth to her dream, her entire nine-and-a-half month pregnancy—similar in length to humans—had been building toward this moment. This is what she was created for—to produce milk and reproduce in a fruitful manner.

Then something happened. As soon as she lay down in the grasslands, coyotes caught scent that this heifer was vulnerable to attack. Vultures lazily circled overhead, waiting for seconds.

Her dream was in jeopardy because of her weakened state. After she gave birth, coyotes warily moved closer. They saw how the weakened mother couldn't get to her feet to protect her newborn calf, which struggled to find its legs. In a flash, the predators pounced, latching their sharp teeth into the calf's hindquarters. The pack of coyotes mauled the newborn while Mama looked on, too feeble to protect her calf. Within minutes, the coyotes devoured half the calf, destroying the first-time mother's dream.

Dreams have a way of becoming nightmares. That was true for Joseph, of course, but if you look at every great man and great woman in the Bible who were asked to do something or be part of something far greater than themselves, that dream almost always turned out to be a nightmare. Think of Noah hearing God's command to build a humongous ark and stopping everything to follow that dream—and the people living around him making his life miserable with taunts and insults. Think of Moses realizing that the dream God gave him—at the burning bush—to lead the Israelites out of Egypt turned to sorrow when God's chosen people were delivered and then subsequently fell into sin and idolatry.

Here's what we've learned through our lives and by talking to others: if you have a God-given dream and speak it and believe it, don't be surprised if your dream enters the nightmare zone.

When I heard from the Lord about being a Joseph, I would never had imagined that I would be diagnosed with cancer, the most feared and dreaded disease on the planet. Serious life-threatening diseases and unexpected deaths happen. We've heard tragic stories where the mother lost a child at birth. Honeymooning couples losing a spouse in the first week of marriage. Husbands losing jobs. When you have a God-given dream, you have to understand that there are coyotes and vultures waiting to steal your dream.

When we were moving to Missouri, we shared this dream with friends and acquaintances. I can remember the excitement in their eyes when we told them about the adventure on which we were going to embark. When Nicki and I described our plans at public seminars, people in attendance got genuinely excited for us.

At the same time, we moved with our eyes open. We expected difficulties uprooting a family of five, with three children eight and under, and moving from a warm weather state to the Midwest, where they have this thing called "winter." We weren't used to the bone-chattering cold and subzero temperatures day after day. Nor did we expect Beyond Organic to struggle and go through adversities and trials. But we persevered because we knew we were living God's dream for us.

We don't know what God intends for all those dealing with trials and tribulations in their lives, but we do know that in order for God to be God, and in order for our dreams to become reality, we have to be ready to experience circumstances that can only be described as nightmares.

That happened to me (Dr. Pete) right after I had my encounter with Jesus in the hotel room in Arusha, Tanzania. Some of our team members who were *not* there that evening heard about my experience, so they tried to recreate it a couple of nights later by asking various team members to sit on the edge of a hotel bed and be prayed for by the group.

When nothing happened out of the ordinary, then my experience must have not been real, some said. Others declared they were more qualified or deserving than me. I wasn't going to argue against that logic, but I failed to see their point.

Amidst the negativity, I came to realize that God chose me and He chooses others to have these types of dreams and experiences. I was not any more qualified or deserving; it just happened. Sure, I said, "Give it to me" when someone in that hotel room suggested that they pray for someone for ten minutes, but that was out of faith that God would listen to their prayers and do something "extraordinary" in my life.

The kingdom of God is not about earning and deserving a spiritual experience over someone else, it's about believing and receiving. I *believed* that God would do something in my life when I said, "Give it to me." I *received* the Joseph Blessing when that happened. Since then, I've been reminded countless times that it didn't happen because of me but rather in spite of me. It's only the grace of God being fulfilled in a person's life that brings God glory, not ourselves!

What I've learned from this experience is that the fruit of one's life will always speak louder than the words coming out of his or her lips. There was no reason to concern myself with critics. Instead, I gravitated toward friends and family members who had wise counsel waiting for me. I could and did trust them to speak truth to me in love.

Their advice was on point: Stay the course that the Lord of the Universe presented to me in Tanzania about reaching 100 million souls for Christ and one billion through the media.

And here's another thought: Why would I ever doubt why He spoke those words to me?

All I have to do is remain faithful and step through the doors He opens for me to preach His word to a hurting world that's hungry to hear about the Hope of Hopes.

A Promise Made

What's striking about Joseph's story is how it's both expansive and integral to God's plan to rescue the world, a plan that started with God's promise to Joseph's ancestor, Abraham.

Abraham was told repeatedly that he would be the father of many nations. God pledged that He would make Abraham into a great nation whose descendants would be as numerous as the stars of the sky and the grains of sand on the seashore.

Abraham made some mistakes, but ultimately Abraham and Sarah were given evidence of their dream in Isaac. Years later, at a time when Abraham was climbing the mountain with his son, Isaac, the patriarch took each labored step with a heavy heart, knowing he was heading toward a destination that would involve his son's death.

The Bible doesn't tell us what Abraham was feeling during that time. These days, there'd be a news helicopter overhead and cameramen in towers along the route and a Go-Pro camera at the mountaintop altar so that we could see the anguish on Abraham's face. Maybe it's just as well that we can use our imagination. But try to imagine what was churning inside of Abraham. The Lord had told him to sacrifice his son—the one who needed to live in order to fulfill God's promise to Abraham that he would be the "father of many nations."

We would imagine that while walking toward Mt. Moriah, Abraham's only thought was, *I wish I had never had Isaac.* A life of obedience to God had turned into a living nightmare because with his own hand he was to kill the dream God had given him.

We know how Abraham bound his son to the altar and raised his hand, gripping a sharp blade, when an angel of the Lord stopped him from stabbing his frightened son to death. Think about this: without Joseph's nightmare, the Joseph Blessing wouldn't be there. Sometimes we must go through this "dark night of the soul," the valley of the shadow of death, in order for God to instill in us that we are worthy in carrying out the dream.

Maybe you've had thoughts like this:

- *I wish I had never said this.*

- *I wish I had never moved here.*

- *I wish I had never gotten married.*

- *I wish I had never gotten pregnant.*

If you've been faithful in proclaiming and following your God-given dream and you're thinking about turning back, high-tailing it out of there, then there's a good chance that it is indeed a dream from God. The way you know the difference is that you go through this nightmare, through this valley of the shadow of death, through this dark night of the soul, and you continue to proclaim, *That's the dream God gave me.*

And that's the way you navigate a nightmare. Remember this Scripture from Psalms 23:4: "Yea, though I walk through the valley of the shadow of death, I will fear no evil; for You are with me."

It's in this fiery trial, this nightmare, where everything seems to be against us that the Lord develops our greatest strength within us. As James 1:2-4 reminds us, "My brethren, count it all joy when you fall into various trials, knowing that the testing of your faith produces patience. But let patience have its perfect work, that you may be perfect and complete, lacking nothing."

Especially a dream from the Lord.

THE JOSEPH BLESSING PRAYER

Lord, You said in Your word that fiery trials will come. I ask You to harden me to the difficulties that surround me and hold me up with Your victorious right hand. I thank You that no weapon formed against me will prosper, and I thank You that what the enemy means for my harm You will turn around and use for Your glory. I declare if God be for me, nothing can come against me.

8

DON'T BIRTH ISHMAEL

Now Sarai, Abram's wife, had borne him no children. And she had an Egyptian maidservant whose name was Hagar. So Sarai said to Abram, "See now, the Lord has restrained me from bearing children. Please, go in to my maid; perhaps I shall obtain children by her." And Abram heeded the voice of Sarai. Then Sarai, Abram's wife, took Hagar her maid, the Egyptian, and gave her to her husband Abram to be his wife, after Abram had dwelt ten years in the land of Canaan. So he went in to Hagar, and she conceived. And when she saw that she had conceived, her mistress became despised in her eyes (Genesis 16:1-4).

FOUR HUNDRED YEARS BEFORE JOSEPH, ABRAHAM LIVED IN the city of Ur, a bustling metropolis near the ancient coastline of the Persian Gulf. Abram, as he was known in those days, was repulsed by the idolatry and sin that he saw in Ur. He was a man of faith who had come to know the one true and living God.

And then Abram had a direct encounter with the Lord, which is related in Genesis 12:1-3:

> *Get out of your country from your family and from your father's house, to a land that I will show you. I will make you a great nation; I will bless you and make your name great; and you shall be a blessing. I will bless those who bless you, and I will curse him who curses you; and in you all the families of the earth shall be blessed.*

Abram obediently pulled up roots and moved his clan and possessions to the land of Canaan, much like American pioneers who had "Westward Ho!" painted on their wagons in the mid-19th century. One of the jumping-off points for the American westward migration was St. Joseph, Missouri, 350 miles from Koshnokong. Pioneering families camped out in St. Joseph in late winter and waited for spring to arrive because their animals needed grassy fields to fuel their race across the Great Plains. If they were headed to California's fertile Central Valley, they had a journey of 1,666 miles ahead of them.

The passage from Ur to Canaan wasn't as far but far more arduous. Abram's route took him and his clan along a "fertile crescent" up the Euphrates River and down the Jordan Valley, a roundabout route that avoided desert sands but made for 1,100 difficult miles. We can't imagine how difficult it was to travel such a great distance somewhere around 2000 B.C., when Abram's exodus took place. In ancient times, they walked every step of the way. Pack animals carried their possessions because there were no covered wagons.

Abram and his traveling party arrived in Canaan, where the lands were already occupied by the Canaanites. Abram didn't have the firepower to take possession of the land, so he moved south and "pitched his tent with Bethel on the west and Ai on the east" (Genesis 12:8). Then he moved even further south into the Negev, a waterless and barren land in the Arabian Peninsula. He and his flocks stayed near the edge of civilization, barely hanging on. Is this where God was leading him? He had to be asking that question. A whole lot had happened to Abram, but he believed in the dream the Lord gave him so much that we're told that God "credited it to him as righteousness" (Genesis 15:6 NIV).

Life got desperate from the lack of good pasture, however. When there was severe famine in the land, Abram moved everyone to Egypt to get food. Sound familiar?

Abram eventually returned to Canaan and took possession of the land. We're told that Abram was very rich in livestock, silver, and gold. "Then He [the Lord] brought him [Abram] outside and said, 'Look now toward heaven, and count the stars if you are able to number them.' And He said to him, 'So shall your descendants be'" (Genesis 15:5).

The problem was that his wife, Sarai, had not conceived, and they were both getting up there in years. We're going to skip through some details of a complicated story, but because Sarai couldn't get pregnant, she took things into her own hands and offered Abram her Egyptian slave girl, Hagar. Sarai, motivated by her love for Abram and desire to "help" God out of a sticky situation—because everyone knew that the Lord had made a covenant with Abram to become the father of "many nations"—endorsed the union.

The result was the birth of Ishmael, who was a handful from the get-go, just as the Angel of the Lord said to Hagar during her pregnancy in Genesis 16:11-12:

> *Behold, you are with child, and you shall bear a son. You shall call his name Ishmael, because the Lord has heard your affliction. He shall be a wild man; his hand shall be against every man, and every man's hand against him. And he shall dwell in the presence of all his brethren.*

The birth of Ishmael created incredible strife between Abraham and Sarah, as they came to be called by the Lord. When Sarah incredibly became pregnant at the age of 90 and gave birth to Isaac, Ishmael mocked her son as they grew up. The strife became so real that Hagar and her son were sent away when the boy was old enough.

So let's backtrack here. Abraham had a vision that he would be the father of many nations. We know it was from God. Sarah was barren, so she suggested that Abram have a child through Hagar, a servant. She looked at the situation he was in and said, "Obviously, this having-a-child-thing isn't going to happen." Abraham went along with Sarah's idea and birthed Ishmael, but birthing Ishmael wasn't the fulfillment of the promise that God gave Abraham, of him having more descendants than the stars in the sky.

So, how many times have you looked at God's grand vision for you and said, "That's impossible. I have to do my part here. What can I do to help bring forth this dream God has for me?"

Your help is unnecessary and unneeded. At the end of the day, it won't work because what you're doing is birthing Ishmael and not trusting God for the outcome of your dream.

I (Dr. Pete) have had moments where I've wanted to "birth Ishmael." When I've been busy seeing patients, wondering how I'm going to pay my bills, I've gone through some tough patches when I said to myself, *Lord, this doesn't look anything like a billion souls.*

If I'm doing the math, I'm thinking that I should be doing sixteen evangelistic crusades a year and buying up enough TV time to drive the Tony Robbins and old Jack LaLanne infomercials off the air. Then there are the naysayers out there, the ones who say, *You're not qualified. Who says you're an evangelist? You've never been to seminary. You're a chiropractor. You're not even a pastor.*

The struggle for me is not birthing Ishmael in this process. I do that by reminding myself what the Lord has told me: I've called you to be a part of winning a billion souls, but I've also called you to be faithful one day at a time and be a steward over your life. Be a blessing where you are.

Attempting to walk in the Joseph Blessing by my might and power won't work and won't bear fruit. Unless the Lord builds the house, it's built in vain.

THE FOLLY OF MAKING THINGS HAPPEN

Let me (Jordan) follow up on what Dr. Pete had to say about birthing Ishmael.

Okay, let's say you receive the dream. You speak the dream. You walk in integrity. Some people are excited, some people are against you. Either way, perhaps you begin to believe your own hype.

You make sacrifices, and you believe that God is going to honor them. Then comes the nightmare, followed by the hovering vultures while the dream killers circle around.

Under such a scenario, most people will do one of two things. They will either turn back and retreat on their dream, or they will do something that is possibly even worse and believe that God can't accomplish the dream without them.

When Joseph was in prison due to the unfair accusation of Potiphar's wife, he met the chief cup bearer and baker, who needed their off-the-wall dreams interpreted. It's easy to surmise that Joseph had grown weary from years and years of prison and slavery and servitude—maybe eight, nine, or ten years by now.

When he interpreted the cup bearer's dream, Joseph said: "You will be raised up in three days to hold the king's cup again. And when you do, remember me." Joseph didn't put his first trust in God to get him out of prison. He asked the cup bearer for a favor, a quid pro quo. *I did this for you. You do this for me.*

When Abraham was told to look at the stars in the sky and the sand on the seashore and so shall his descendants be, Abraham believed God. Yet he was willing to risk everything by lying to the Egyptian pharaoh that his wife, Sarai, was really his sister. What could have happened in that case? The pharaoh could have conceived the baby with Sarah, so therefore he wouldn't be Abraham's son, meaning God wouldn't have worked the miracle.

But Abraham did something even worse. Through collusion with Sarah, he conceived a child with Hagar and birthed Ishmael, which caused some of the greatest struggles throughout the history of biblical times and right through to today and even our future.

There is a great temptation when you have a dream—you speak it, you believe it, you live it—but it turns into a nightmare and then you see things not happen. So you figure, *I know God said He would make the dream come about, but just in case He doesn't come through, I better do this myself.*

You are not going to retreat. You are going to stick with it even if you're thinking, *Maybe God did not mean what He said.* Nothing is impossible with God, absolutely nothing.

So many times during my journey, particularly with the excruciating difficulties hitting Beyond Organic, I looked at an open night sky and said: "Look at the stars, so shall the mission marketers be, so shall the message of Beyond Organic get out there."

I really thought that I had to do something or make something happen so that Beyond Organic would be successful. As much as I tried by my own might, we struggled and struggled. There were so many setbacks. I thought, *Maybe it's not really going to happen with this company I started. Maybe I heard wrong.*

But God will do something often just in the nick of time, because He is never early and He is never late. I have faith that He will bring forth something that I couldn't have asked for or couldn't have imagined. Something that I did not know how to do in my own strength. His plans for Beyond Organic are just that—His plans. He's in control of the outcome.

I was cognizant of the fact that I can't birth Ishmael while I wait for God to act. I waited for the Lord to open doors, and He did when He provided an opportunity for Beyond Organic to partner with a much larger company through the same channel in May 2014.

By most estimations, Beyond Organic had been highly successful in getting products to thousands of people each month. A small, passionate army of mission marketers and a powerful group of products paved the way. However, I built the infrastructure of Beyond Organic for much greater sales and much larger growth. Over the course of 2013, we literally set a half dozen dates to close down the company. Boy, am I glad I didn't take matters into my own hands because He had a partner waiting in the wings.

I'm glad I knew in the back of my mind that I couldn't make something happen on my own, so I rested the situation in Jesus' hands. As I share this story today, I'm convinced that God will do everything in His timing and in His way. I still believe God is going to bring about what He promised me in my dream. I still believe the Beyond Organic message will reach the ends of the earth. And, of course, I believe God will use me to provide for the physical needs of His children in the coming perilous times.

I see a path forward now that I couldn't have imagined before, and it's because I didn't take things into my own hands and birth Ishmael.

Our advice to those seeking the Joseph Blessing is to stay the course and trust the dream that God gave you. Most likely, your dream will be tested and your dream will take you to places you never thought possible, but the Lord is asking you not to rely on your own strength at this time, but on Him.

THE JOSEPH BLESSING PRAYER

Lord, grant me the grace to resist the lie that my ways are better than Your ways. Forgive me for striving in my own strength. Glorify Yourself in my weakness. As Jeremiah said, "Blessed is he who puts his confidence in the Lord, whose hope is in the Lord." Work through me to accomplish Your purpose, Your divine will for my life. Thank You for the opportunity to abide in You and bear much fruit.

9

LAY DOWN YOUR ISAAC

Now it came to pass after these things that God tested Abraham, and said to him, "Abraham!" And he said, "Here I am." Then He said, "Take now your son, your only son Isaac, whom you love, and go to the land of Moriah, and offer him there as a burnt offering on one of the mountains of which I shall tell you" (Genesis 22:1-2).

ABRAHAM MARRIED WELL WHEN HE CHOSE A BEAUTY NAMED Sarah to be his wife. He didn't have to go far to find her; Scripture tells us that Sarah was Abraham's half-sister—the daughter of his father and a different mother. She was so pretty that she turned Pharaoh's head...when she was sixty-five years old. Even at an age when she qualified as a senior citizen, Pharaoh desired her for his harem, as did a king named Abimelech years after him.

As much as Abraham and Sarah loved each other, she could not conceive a child. At the age of ninety, one of the great miracles of the Bible happened. Long after she had presumably gone through menopause—probably a good forty years—Sarah was with child. She was overjoyed—and probably more amazed than we are three thousand years later. Sarah knew the stakes as well as the promise God made to Abraham—that an entire nation would come through her and Abraham.

Imagine, then, how Sarah and Abraham felt, years after the birth of Isaac, when Abraham was told by God to take their only son to the region of Moriah and sacrifice him as a burnt offering atop one of the mountains. This was an astounding commandment because Isaac embodied the love and adoration of his parents as well as the future of a great nation.

Most everyone knows what happened the moment Abraham lifted a knife to slay his son as a sacrifice. The Angel of the Lord said, "Do not lay your hand on the lad, or do anything to him; for now I know that you fear God, since you have not withheld your son, your only son, from Me" (Genesis 22:12).

Abraham turned and saw a ram caught in the thicket. He captured the ram and offered it up as a burnt offering instead of his son.

Let me tell you why this story of Abraham laying down his Isaac resonates with me (Jordan) beyond the illustration of total obedience and total dependence. Ever since 2008,

I've known that God has given me a dream to buy farm and ranch land, springs, livestock, and seeds to provide food and sustenance for others. A company was formed called Beyond Organic, and new products were developed. One of them was a wonderful cultured dairy beverage known as Amasai, a nutritious smoothie-like drink with more than thirty probiotics.

I mentioned in the last chapter how Beyond Organic, as a company, struggled and lost a considerable amount of money during its first two years of operations. I'll be frank here: I'm used to seeing a company that I'm running experience meteoric success. The sales trajectory is always expected to be up.

And yet Beyond Organic was running deep in the red. How could this happen? We knew what we were doing was in the Lord's will. His leading to Missouri was unmistakable. And yet this was turning out to be like Abraham's walk with Isaac to the mountains of Moriah. As Beyond Organic made every effort to succeed, the numbers kept getting worse and worse. Those of us closely involved with Beyond Organic were at the end of ourselves. We were rapidly approaching a point where nothing was left that we could do to save the company.

After much deliberation and prayer, I knew what the Lord was directing me to do: plunge the knife into Beyond Organic. Kill the company. Let it go.

And emotionally, that's where we were—ready to close the doors. But then God provided a ram in a thicket. He found a way for Beyond Organic to continue—through a partnership with a company known as Youngevity Essential Life Sciences. Beyond Organic would still share its unique message and provide amazing products, but now the company would be part of the bigger Youngevity family.

What happened with Youngevity wasn't anything I could do by my power or might. Everything came together after I made the decision to carry my dream to the altar and was seriously ready to plunge the knife. When God showed up, He told me that it was not by might nor by power but by His spirit that He would keep the Beyond Organic dream alive.

Knowing there was nothing I could do was actually freeing. I didn't have to go through my daily life crippled with worry. I didn't have to envision the faces of the people who were faithful to share the Beyond Organic message from the very beginning as mission marketers—and seeing their own dreams dashed. I didn't have to think about the thousands of people who benefitted greatly from consuming the products that they had come to depend on, suddenly finding themselves living without those awesome foods. I had given up everything to the Lord and emotionally let it go. But by the spirit of God, He gave it back to us.

Even though my dream is alive, it's not fulfilled, but we have a better platform for sharing our message of health and hope, expanding our mission marketers, and continuing to produce products that can change lives.

In some ways, I feel like Joseph when he was released from prison. No one was bowing down to him yet, but his future was about to change the future of the world.

ANOTHER VIEW

When I (Dr. Pete) think of times in my life where there's been the death of a vision, the Lord has always reminded me that I'm merely doing what I've been called to do. If something doesn't work or I don't have the right relationships with someone who can help me, I lay it down at the Lord's feet. I've been amazed at the doors that have opened up wide or the encouragement I've received.

I've recently been at the point where I've said, *Lord, I can't do it anymore. I've done everything I can. It's either You, or it's not. If You've called me to India and the world, You must open the doors.*

That's when I met certain key leaders in the Billy Graham Evangelistic Association who offered to network with me on crusades in India. They were like divine appointments. I could have never put these relationships together. Billy Graham is widely known as the greatest evangelist of the 20th century, and now some of his children, grandchildren, and close associates are linking arms with me! Three or four other well-known ministries have also graciously offered their counsel and support.

You can test Him on this: When you pray with a genuine heart, *Lord, I give it to you, I lay down my Isaac,* He will respond in this fashion: *Now I can finally do something in your life.*

When you want to see God work in your life after He's given you a dream, don't be surprised when things don't seem to work out the way you think they will. You very well may have to sacrifice your dream—your Isaac. But I'm supremely confident that God—the one who gave you your dream—will bring it to pass and whatever anyone or any circumstance meant for bad, no matter how many people who are around you are unrighteous, you will thrive.

I believe the God who called Himself the *I am that I am*, who was and is and is to come, the Alpha and Omega, the beginning and the end, will triumph and cause your God-given dream to change the world.

THE JOSEPH BLESSING PRAYER

Lord, teach me to deny myself, my agenda, and my plans. As the apostle Paul said, "I am crucified with Christ, nevertheless, not I who lives, but Christ lives within me." The life I now live in the flesh, I live by faith in the Son of God. I thank You that when all hope seems to be lost You are God, and You will make a way where there seems to be no other way. I lay down my life and my dream at Your altar as a living sacrifice. Today, may I know the power of Your resurrection.

10

WALK IN HIS SPIRIT

So Joseph answered Pharaoh, saying, "It is not in me; God will give Pharaoh an answer of peace" (Genesis 41:16).

OUR GOAL, BY THE TIME YOU FINISH *THE JOSEPH BLESSING*, is that there be a fresh revelation in your spirit. Remind yourself that He is the author and finisher of your faith. He is the first and last and the beginning and the end.

Be it unto us according to Jesus Christ. You are His favorite. He is the one who gave you the dream. He is the one who placed it within your spirit. He is the one who sustains you in the midst of fiery trials. Be it unto us now according to Jesus Christ, your El-Shaddai, your God of more than enough. Be it unto you according to your Jehovah Rapha, your healer, and your Jehovah Jireh, your provider. Be it unto you according to He who does exceedingly, abundantly above all that we could ask for or imagine.

I (Dr. Pete) have been thinking these thoughts as I walk in His spirit while seeking to walk out the Joseph Blessing in my life. I know what's happened over the last ten years is because of my divine appointment in a Tanzanian hotel room. I'm comfortable knowing that I'm not equipped to reach a billion souls for Christ through the media, but I'm called to do so. I've asked the Lord to equip me because He's the one who called me to this harvest, which takes the responsibility off of myself. Two verses replay in my mind:

- "Blessed is the man who trusts in the Lord, and whose hope is the Lord" (Jeremiah 17:7).

- "My help comes from the Lord, who made heaven and earth" (Psalms 121:2).

Meditating on these verses sets my mind on things above and not on things of the earth. I was reflecting on this in my prayer time recently when the Lord told me, *Quit dipping below the clouds.*

Did I hear right? "What do you mean, Lord, quit dipping below the clouds?" I asked.

Quit fighting spiritual battles with earthly armor. Come up with Me, high above all principalities and powers, where you're seated with Me in heavenly places with Christ Jesus, where the battle is not yours anymore but where the battle is Mine and the victory is already won.

What the Lord was reminding me was that there is a place of rest for the people of God, where we no longer have to dip below the clouds, where we are buffeted by the winds of change and the storms of life. We no longer have to fight spiritual battles with earthly armor. We can simply come up with Him—above the stormy weather—and know that He has smoothed our way as our advocate. He is a God who will fight with us and for us. The battle is no longer ours when we're above the clouds with Him. The victory has already been won.

But all of us will consistently have the temptation to fight spiritual battles with earthly armor. There have been times when I've certainly charged forth, sword held up high, and been brutally defeated. The Lord says, "How's that going for you?"

My reply: "Not very well."

"Then I bid you to come up with Me, where the victory is already won."

There's also a component of rest for the people of God. When we come up with Him, we will receive rest. He knows we didn't choose the assignment. Instead, He chose us and appointed us to bear great fruit. Supernatural grace is released when all we have is our dependence on Him.

There's another vision I had with the Lord that I must share. It happened when I found myself walking on a body of water with Jesus. My first reaction was, "Wow, this is awesome." I was holding Jesus' hand and walking on the water, feeling proud of myself.

We kept walking until we found ourselves in the middle of a body of water. He said, "Turn around," but I couldn't see the shoreline. Then He said, "Try to get back."

That's when I began to sink, setting off panic that I could drown.

He spoke to me again. *I'm taking you to a place where you will see the impossible and see the miraculous, but you better hold on to Me for dear life. To walk out the call I have for your life, it has to be Me. If you go out on it alone, you will sink and drown. Trust in Me with all your heart, not with your own understanding, and I will direct your paths. Do not be wise in your own eyes. Fear Me and depart from evil.*

To walk in His spirit is a wonderful thing. If this concept is new to you, then my encouragement to you is to ask the Lord to take baby steps with you.

When you're holding His hand, you can be sure you're headed in the right direction.

AN UNEXPECTED PHONE CALL

Here's an example of how God worked in my life. A couple of years ago, I was in India, planning an upcoming evangelistic crusade due to happen in a few short months. I was waiting for a flight at Kolkata Airport, getting ready for an intra-India flight to Nagaland to speak at an event celebrating Christianity being established by my great-grandparents one hundred years earlier.

My speaking crusades are supported by Matthew 10 International Ministries, a non-profit organization based in the States that raises money to pay for our evangelistic work, including the cost to stage crusades and pay for the travel to foreign lands as well as support our efforts to care for widows and orphans. That morning in India, I sat in an airport lounge with Tom Bennett, one of our board members, and talked about the budget for the upcoming crusade.

"Dude, it's go time," I said to Tom. "I know the Srikakulam crusade is what we're supposed to do, but the finances are just not there. What are we going to say to Bishop Ernest?"

Tom didn't have a good answer because there was no answer. Our fundraising efforts had fallen woefully short. We kibitzed back and forth, but it was apparent to us that it was going to take a miracle to pull off this crusade. I told Tom that we needed to pray.

"Lord, I give it to You," I whispered. "I don't know what I'm going to do."

My iPhone chirped. I looked down and saw that Jordan had reached out to me with a text message that said this: "Nicki and I want to support you. What does the upcoming crusade cost? How much do you need?"

It was late evening in the United States when I (Jordan) sent Dr. Pete that text. Nicki and I were sitting in bed, talking and reading, when she looked up from the book in her hands. "We need to give money to support Pete," she said.

I know my wife pretty well, and when she says, "We need to give money to Pete," she's not making a suggestion or talking off the top of her head. What she's saying is that God is leading us to support Pete in a significant way.

Pete and Matthew 10 Ministries were on Nicki's mind quite a bit at that time because we were planning to accompany him and his team to India for his next crusade. Months earlier, Pete had been in South Florida and stopped by the house for a visit. When Nicki heard him describe what a typical trip was like—open-air evangelistic events, salvations, healings—she wanted to sign up that night. "We're going!" she declared.

What Nicki said didn't surprise me. She's always had a heart for missions and evangelism and certainly children. And then we found ourselves relaxing in bed before we turned out the lights, and Nicki saying, "We need to give toward this crusade."

Long story short, we felt led to make up the gap in Dr. Pete's budget for the upcoming crusade. We made the decision not realizing the great need Pete and Matthew 10 had. We may not have known the need, but our God did. We just wanted to help out, so we asked Pete what the shortfall was.

Pete texted back a certain figure that would fully fund that crusade. We were all in. As far as we were concerned it was the Lord's money.

I (Dr. Pete) remember texting this message back to Jordan: *You don't know what you've done. I'm crying.*

You see, only 25 percent of the budget had been raised at that time. That wasn't going to be nearly enough, and in my mind at the time we would surely need to cancel the crusade. I'd birthed Ishmael in the past when I refinanced my house to raise the money, but that option was no longer available. We were personally tapped out.

Nicki and I felt led by the Spirit that day, which imprinted an important lesson on both of us. When you're walking in His spirit, He will use you to meet the needs of others and give you the desires of your heart.

THE JOSEPH BLESSING PRAYER

Lord, thank You that my life is not my own. Lead me by Your spirit in paths of righteousness that honor You. I surrender my life to You completely and fully. I declare that You who began a good work in me will bring it to completion. You will accomplish and establish Your plans for my life not by power, not by might, but by Your spirit, O God. Thank You that Your blessings are not too good to be true, but are just the beginning. I declare according to Your Word that there is no end to Your increase in my life.

11

ALLOW GOD TO TAKE OVER

By the God of your father who will help you, and by the Almighty who will bless you with blessings of heaven above, blessings of the deep that lies beneath, blessings of the breasts and of the womb. The blessings of your father have excelled the blessings of my ancestors, up to the utmost bound of the everlasting hills. They shall be on the head of Joseph, and on the crown of him who was separate from his brothers (Genesis 49:25-26).

I (JORDAN) DESCRIBED IN CHAPTER 6 HOW MY SON, JOSHUA, eight years old at the time, experienced a series of eight dreams. In one of them, God spoke to Joshua and told him that it was time to build a children's home in Missouri.

That was quite a dream the Lord gave him because after Nicki and I finalized the purchase of the Missouri ranch and farm homestead, it was never our intention to live there. Like I said earlier, the plan was to visit every few months, check on things, let the kids get their hands dirty feeding goats and chickens, but we were used to the trappings of suburbia—private schools, recreational sports, shopping at malls, church life, the beach, and social engagements.

And then we let God take over.

During the summer of 2012, Nicki and I were in church on Sunday morning, as we normally are. Four years earlier, the Lord had moved us from an awesome megachurch with four campuses and 20,000 members, where we'd been active members for thirteen years, to a church plant with thirty-five people that rented an elementary school auditorium. In four short years, though, we had to move to a new building because we had grown to between four hundred and five hundred members.

It was great to be in Generation Church that particular morning as we had been traveling for nearly two months. The church seemed more full, the worship band seemed to sound better, and I even thought to myself, *I love this church. I love our friends. I love this city, and I love this life.* It was at that moment when the Lord spoke to me as we stood there, lifting our voices to Him during worship. There's no other way to describe it, but I knew He was speaking to me and relaying an important message.

I bowed my head, overcome with the experience. Tears welled up in my eyes. Then I felt a bump in my ribs.

"Are you okay?" Nicki knew I never cry during a service.

I nodded, then shook my head. I wasn't okay because something supernatural had happened. "The Lord just spoke to me, but I don't think I can get the words out. I'm going to type what He said on the BlackBerry," I said.

My fingers worked furiously: *The Lord says we're leaving here soon. Not only will we have a children's home in Missouri, but we'll start a church and a school. We're not going alone. People are going with us.*

Now it was Nicki's turn to cry.

This experience happened in July 2012. Believe me, in the aftermath, Nicki and I held long discussions about what the Lord had spoken to me. This was serious stuff—a decision to uproot a family and move a great distance to a 4,000-acre ranch that was miles from…well, civilization.

Nicki even joked about asking the Lord, "Is there anything we can do in Florida? Just so You know, we love it here." Even though rural Missouri was *not* where she wanted to live, she had a great attitude about moving because she knew I had heard directly from the Lord, who had a megaphone in His hand instead of His usual still, small voice.

"I knew we had to be willing to do this," she said. "That's why during a time of questioning the Lord and asking, *Why me? I feel like I'm being punished*, that the Lord said to me, *I asked you because I knew you'd say yes. Actually, what I'm asking you to do is a privilege, not a punishment.*"

It's hard to turn your back on a direct message from the Lord. In fact, I'll put it in different terms. Nicki and I had to take our hands off the wheel and let God take over.

But we also heard Him saying something else to us: *Just tell people you're moving. Don't expect anyone to join you. Don't try to talk anybody into going. Just tell your friends what the Lord is doing and see what happens.*

That's what we did. If we felt like the Lord was directing us to tell certain friends and family about our plans, that's what we did. If He didn't give us that leading, we let it go. In our vision for the future, though, we saw certain people joining us. Some of them came with us, and some didn't. Again, it was all in the Lord's hands.

We were open to moving at any time, but we decided to set a deadline for early June after the kids finished school the following May.

Although the move wasn't easy and certainly took an attitude adjustment, we have seen numerous blessings in our lives. We could have grumbled about the subzero cold that gripped Missouri during the Winter of '14, the lack of a four-wheel drive car to drive on icy roads, or the isolation that surrounded us—and, of course, all of the trials and tribulations that I shared earlier in this book. Instead, we reminded ourselves that God had led us to Missouri for a reason, through a dream and a vision, and we weren't going to whine like the Hebrews did when they left Egypt.

We took comforts large and small from where we could find them. Raising egg-laying chickens was a treat, although we learned that roosters like to crow *before* dawn's first light. Enjoying fresh milk from our goats and cows as the basis for amazing raw smoothies was awesome. Eating delicious whole grain pasta dishes topped with a rich organic tomato sauce from homegrown tomatoes and beef from our grass-fed cattle couldn't get any better.

But in the grand scheme of things, we trusted God because He was driving the bus. Today as I write this, I may not be the second most important man in the kingdom as Joseph was in Egypt, but God has delivered me miraculously in ways I can't even describe. When things seemed to be completely out of control and I had nowhere to turn, God showed up and He simply took over.

It's interesting for me (Dr. Pete) to hear Jordan share this because I had a dream in which the Lord said, "Quit driving the bus."

Here's what happened in my dream. I was crossing an intersection in a large metropolitan city, much like Minneapolis. Shiny skyscrapers blocked the sun. The sidewalk was teeming with people busy walking to shops, their work, or toward home.

It must have been rush hour because I saw a long line at a bus stop. I knew I had to get somewhere—I wasn't sure where—but I figured I was at the right bus stop.

I spoke to the first person in line. "Is this the bus I need to be on?"

"Yes, but the bus isn't here yet," he said, stating the obvious. "You'll have to wait like everyone else, so be patient. Don't worry. You'll get to the destination that you're called to reach."

There was something "off" about that reply, but I wasn't sure what it was. Then my eyes looked across the street. I saw a wildly painted bus parked across the street. The multicolored bus reminded me of the psychedelic ones driven by hippies in the sixties. Joseph's "Technicolor dreamcoat" was tame compared to this.

I didn't want to wait for the bus I was supposed to take. I wanted to get on the bus across the boulevard. The fact that it was pointed in the opposite direction didn't register with me.

I crossed the intersection and walked to the bus stop. No line over here. The front door was wide open. I looked in— and saw the seats were taken with schoolchildren and their backpacks. The driver's seat was empty—but the key was in the ignition.

I looked to my left and my right. I didn't see a driver taking a break anywhere. Without thinking, I stepped inside and sat in the driver's seat. Gripped the steering wheel. Imagined what it would be like to take off.

My hand reached for the ignition, and the diesel engine fired up. I looked in my side mirror, and when I saw a gap, I swung into traffic. The kids continued to chatter away. They thought they had a new bus driver.

I had never driven a big city bus before, but I kind of like being king of the road. Then I saw my first intersection. I decided to take a right. Don't ask me why. I just felt like it. Then I traveled two more blocks and attempted a left-hand turn. I was sure this would get me to my destination, wherever it was.

The left-hand turn took me into a part of the city I didn't recognize. Everything looked unfamiliar to me. I arrived at a four-way stop sign and decided on a whim to take a left. Now I was really lost. I took rights and lefts, having no idea where I was going. Then I came to a dead end.

The kids stopped making noise. Everyone got real silent. My chest started beating faster as I realized I had put these innocent kids into some sort of danger. I was feeling horrible about what I'd done—

I woke up from my dream, which actually felt like a nightmare.

I went into prayer, and then I asked, "Lord, what was that all about?"

I heard an answer: *The first bus stop where you got in line—that was the destiny for your life. I was driving that bus, but you were too impatient to wait for Me to arrive. Instead, you crossed the street and stole a bus packed with kids because you thought you knew where you were going. You didn't, and that became very evident.*

I felt shamed. God was primed to drive me to my destination, but my impatience had gotten the best of me.

I got back into the same dream a few nights later. Just like the first time, I saw a group of people waiting patiently at a bus stop in the middle of a downtown, surrounded by skyscrapers.

This time I waited, and when the Lord drove up, He allowed the others to get on. When it was my turn, I stepped on.

"I'm glad you waited because My yoke is easy and My burden is light," He said. "On My bus, all you have to do is take a seat, relax, look out the window, and I will take you on a road toward righteousness. I will bring you exactly where you're supposed to be at precisely the right time."

And then my dream ended.

Now that I've had some time to reflect on what the Lord was teaching me, I've come to this conclusion: God has a destiny waiting for me. He birthed it, and He placed it within my spirit.

God is not a replicator or a duplicator. He has a unique destiny waiting for you. All you have to do is be ready to let God drive the bus.

In this book, Jordan and I have shared our dreams and our revelation of what it means to experience the Joseph Blessing. As you can tell, we are passionate about the vision for the future that the Lord has revealed to us. We're not here to say that our dreams are better than yours. What we want you to do is be as passionate as we are about your dream. Get on His bus and see where it takes you.

You might be taken to a stop named "The Joseph Blessing," where you can taste and experience the goodness of God. When you begin to see the manifestation of what God can do and His dream for you coming to fulfillment, there's no end to the increase of God.

He says He will do exceedingly, abundantly above all you could ask, think, or imagine, according to the very power that works within you. Know this: you never have to be ashamed of the blessing of the Lord. He has called you, He has chosen you, and He has appointed you to bear great fruit. It's time to expand your vision and move out the tent pegs because the blessing of the Lord will be released after you've taken possession of the dream and vision He's given you.

The Joseph Blessing is just the beginning, so ask God to give you your dream today.

THE JOSEPH BLESSING PRAYER

Lord, thank You for who You are and for all that You're doing in my life. Thank You that Your blessings are not too good to be true, but are just the beginning. I declare according to Your Word that there is no end to Your increase in my life. You have taken me from the miry clay and have set my feet on a rock and have given me a firm place to stand. I will sing of Your goodness all the rest of my days.

12

WALK IN THE
JOSEPH BLESSING

JOSEPH AND THE ASTONISHING LIFE HE LED IS ONE THAT WE read about, comment on, and hopefully try to imitate 3,500 years later.

Now that's what you call a legacy.

The Joseph Blessing can be yours. We don't care if you're twelve years old or eighty-two years young—God has a dream for you...perhaps today. Whether your dreams are in the future or your dreams have been long forgotten, God is waiting to use you. No matter where you are, this is it. God has a dream for you, and it can change the world.

Neither of us play golf, but we couldn't help but be touched by the story of Bubba Watson, who won the first of two green jackets at Augusta in 2012.

Bubba, a self-effacing golfer in his mid-thirties from Baghdad, Florida, came out of nowhere to win one of golf's major tournaments. After accepting the coveted green jacket in Butler Cabin on the grounds of August National, Bubba told CBS' Jim Nantz and a national audience that, "I've never gotten this far in my dreams."

What an admission of how we all think at one time or another. For Bubba, winning a playoff with a hook shot from the trees was way beyond any hopes or expectations he'd held deep inside, but it happened. For you, it could mean that you're holding back because you think you can't live up to the dream or vision the Lord has given you. But you can, and that's because you have His spirit living inside of you.

When Joseph was released from prison, he was directed to clean up before he would be ushered into Pharaoh's presence, where he'd be asked to interpret a pair of dreams that troubled Pharaoh. After bathing, we're told in Genesis that Joseph was given new garments.

If you've received a fresh revelation from reading *The Joseph Blessing*, maybe it's time to leave your present situation—a prison of sorts—and change *your* garments. Once you freshen up, you can confidently walk into His court with a clean feeling, ready to hear the call of God on your life.

We don't care if your dream is modest or mind-blowing. We don't care if your dream isn't original or different. The important thing is that it's your dream. We urge you to act on the vision God has given you today.

When you take that first step, don't be surprised if you experience the Joseph Blessing very soon in your life.

A CLOSING PRAYER

And now the both of us would like to close *The Joseph Blessing* by praying a prayer over your life. The Lord spoke this prayer to me (Jordan) as I pored over Scripture, determined to understand God's plan of increase for His people.

We encourage you to receive this prayer and to pray it over your life and family daily as you watch the Joseph Blessing manifest in your life:

> *Today we pray that like Job, God would surround you with a hedge of protection and that you would have twice the blessings in the latter part of your life from this day forward.*
>
> *We pray that like Abraham, you would grow wealthy with cattle, gold, and silver.*
>
> *That like Isaac, you'd plant a field and reap a hundredfold harvest.*
>
> *That like Jacob, with wisdom and discernment you would grow your flocks and herds.*
>
> *That like Joseph, the dream that God's given you will be salvation to many.*
>
> *That like Moses, the Lord will reveal Himself to you and show you His glory.*

That like Bazalel, who helped build the tabernacle, the Lord would anoint you for the specific task that He's called you to accomplish.

That like Joshua, God will fill you with the spirit of wisdom.

That like the children of Israel, you'll live in lands that you didn't buy, with barns and houses that you didn't build, filled with things that you didn't purchase, drinking from wells and springs that you didn't know existed, and eating from vineyards and groves that you didn't plant.

That He'd care for your land and water it and enrich it abundantly.

That He'd bless the fruit of your trees, the crops of your land, the grass of your fields, and the calves of your herds.

That He'd bring the spring and autumn rains, softening the land with showers, that your threshing floors will be filled with grain; your vats will overflow with new wine and oil, that your bulls will never fail to breed and your cows will never miscarry, that there would be none sick among you, and none barren, that you would smite a thousand enemies as the Lord fights for you and you would return from battle with silver, gold, bronze, iron, and clothing.

That your sons in their youth will be like well-nurtured plants, and your daughters will be like pillars carved to adorn a palace.

That your sheep will increase by tens of thousands in your fields.

That as you bring the tithe into the storehouse, the Lord will throw open the floodgates of heaven and pour out so much blessing that you will not have enough room for it.

That He will prevent pests from devouring your crops, and the vines in your fields will not cast their fruit.

Then all the nations will call you blessed, for yours will be a delightful land.

That like David, God would give you a blueprint of what He would like you to build for Him.

That like Solomon, He would give you a wise and understanding heart.

That like Uzziah, there would be good men caring for your cattle in the foothills and that you'd have a love and understanding of the soil.

That like Daniel, God would give you ten times the wisdom, favor, understanding, and discernment of all those who don't know Him.

And that like Peter, you'd cast your net on the right side of the boat and catch a multitude of fish.

Not by power, not by might, but by your Spirit, O God.

This is our prayer for you as you walk in your Joseph Blessing today!

ABOUT THE AUTHORS

JORDAN RUBIN is one of America's most recognized and respected natural health experts.

Known as America's Biblical Health Coach, he is a *New York Times* bestselling author of *The Maker's Diet* and 21 additional health titles. An international motivational speaker and host of the weekly television show *Living Beyond Organic* that reaches over 30 million households worldwide, Jordan has lectured on natural health on five continents and forty-eight states in the U.S.

Jordan is the founder of Garden of Life and Beyond Organic, a vertically integrated company specializing in organic foods, beverages, skin and body care, and nutritional supplements. These days, he is farming thousands of organic acres in Missouri, where he resides with his wife, Nicki, and four children.

DR. PETE SULACK is owner of one of the largest and fastest-growing chiropractic clinics in the world. Raised in the Twin Cities of Minneapolis-St. Paul, Dr. Pete attended nearby Bethel College and Northwestern College of Chiropractic. After earning his doctor of chiropractic degree, he and his young family moved to Knoxville, Tennessee, where he opened a practice. Very soon, the practice exploded, and sometimes Dr. Pete treats several hundred patients a day.

In 2004, Dr. Pete accompanied a missions group sharing the Gospel in Tanzania. While in the eastern African country, he received a revelation from the Lord that he was to start preaching the Gospel in foreign lands. He launched a nonprofit ministry called Matthew 10 International, and since then, he's preached in more than fifteen evangelistic crusades in places like India, Argentina, Venezuela, Columbia, and Nigeria.

Dr. Pete and his wife, Stephanie, are the parents of four energetic and athletic boys—Isaiah, Eli, Ashton, and Ezekiel. They make their home in Knoxville.